Don't be late on Monday

Life and work in a Nottingham lace factory

Don't be late on Monday

Mark Ashfield

breedon **books**
PUBLISHING

First published in Great Britain in 2004 by
The Breedon Books Publishing Company Limited
Breedon House, 3 The Parker Centre,
Derby, DE21 4SZ.

Dedication:

For all the family, who might just have suspected
I was once in the lace trade, with my love

ISBN 1 85983 425 6

Printed and bound by Scotprint, Haddington, East Lothian.

Contents

Acknowledgements

Thanks are due to Frank Ashley, Dorothy Ritchie at Nottingham Local Studies and staff at the *Nottingham Evening Post* for their help with the illustrations used in this book. Other illustrations are from the author's own collection.

Preface

THERE never was a firm called Peggoty's in the Nottingham lace trade so far as I know, but the factory recorded in this book – despite the fictionalising of the name – was as real as the cobblestones outside the front doors. I worked for Peggoty's from 1936 to 1959, apart from a four and a half year break during World War Two, and then joined the parent company. I retired in 1984.

Not only did the factory exist, so too did the characters, every one of them. All the incidents recorded are accurate.

The book has been written to give a true picture of life in a lace factory in a vanished age. It was an age that produced (in spite of much hard work and some aspects of life that we wouldn't want to see return) remarkable characters who laboured mightily at their trade and added to the reputation of a once-great industry.

Mark Ashfield

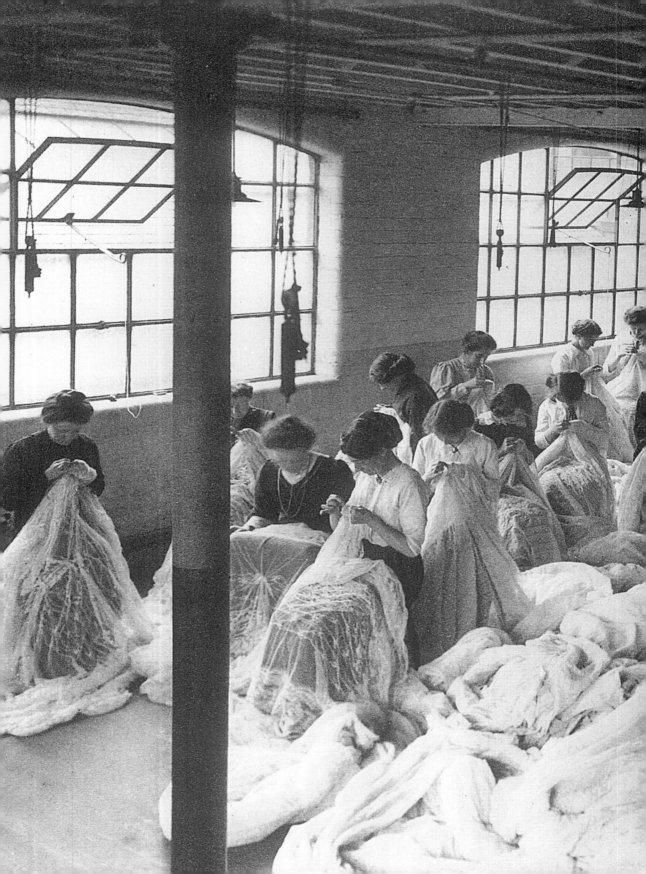

The Old Factory

This car park here,
Crowded off a busy street,
Silences its ghosts by noise.
But they must be there,
Tortured that the high building
Where they spent long years
Has gone, and with it
The craft of centuries.
Where they learned the art
Of making delicate lace,
On which much of the city's fame stands.
But those who daily park here
Look only for a space to squeeze in
Their necessary monsters.
No overnight parking, it warns;
And it is then, in the dark hours,
When the wind blows in the right direction,
There may be heard
The soft clank-clank of machines
Working their gossamer threads
For the sleeping city's
Museum of memories.

'The Old Factory', first printed in
the *Nottingham Evening Post*, in a
section entitled 'The People's
Poems', 25 October 1997.
(Courtesy *Nottingham Evening
Post*)

Chapter One

THAT Saturday evening in early August 1936 is etched needle-sharp in my memory. I was utterly miserable because there was a film showing at the Regent called *Under Two Flags* and I wanted to see it. Victor McLaglen was one of the stars and ever since I'd seen him in *The Informer* I looked forward to his films.

Saturday night at the pictures was the weekly treat for me and my pals. It was even more special because we went to the second house. And that meant we didn't get home until half-past ten. Such were the heady delights of the 1930s, when you were 14, had left school, and were prepared to blow three-quarters of your shilling pocket money on what the locals used to call 'ninepenn'orth o' dark'.

But this particular Saturday Mr McLaglen's celluloid adventures were not shared by me. I'd woken that morning with a sore throat and when I got home from work at two o' clock it was worse. My mother soon had me standing close to the kitchen window, mouth wide, and saying 'Aa-ah'. 'It's your tonsils again,' she said. 'You'll have to have 'em out before you're much older.' And then she looked particularly forbidding and said 'You'd best stay in for the rest of the day.'

'What about the pictures?'

'There's no pictures for you this week, my lad.' And when she said it there was no point in arguing. Looking back, it always seemed to be Mam who made the decisions about what I should do and not do, although I was always conscious of Dad in the background. But he came into the picture only if there was defiance of my mother. It was then that the sergeant handed you over to the sergeant-major.

And so, when my pals called for me I had to pass on the news. But I wanted to know how the Nottinghamshire cricket team was faring against Surrey and was prepared to spend a penny of my pocket money to find out. I persuaded my mother to let me walk down the road to the newsagent's. There was also another reason for wanting to buy an evening paper: I was getting pretty desperate to find a fresh job.

Three great cricketers. I saw C.F. Walters face the
speed and cunning of Voce and Larwood when Worcestershire played Notts.

Out of a population of about 40 million there were near enough three million on the dole and my father was one of them. I remember well enough my mother telling me she couldn't do with two men out of work (a day or two after I'd left school) and my saying she'd no need to worry about me. If I couldn't get a job, I said, I would go into the army. At which point tears came into her eyes and she dashed into the scullery.

But I was lucky enough to get fixed up with a job almost as soon as I left school. That was at Easter and now it was early August; and those four months had nearly killed me. A lad I knew had left school the term before me and was working in Nottingham. He said to me one evening just after I'd left: 'If you want a job come to our place. They are looking for a lad.'

I went as he'd suggested, got the job and found myself the morning after unscrewing stoppers from empty mineral water bottles. The first couple of days were not too bad, although the skin of both hands between thumb and first finger was sore and inflamed. By the end of the first week both hands were blistered and torn and when I started to wear gloves as protection the leather was worn through in no time at all.

Weekends came as a real relief although I was so ashamed of my hands I kept them in my pockets most of the time. I was paid 12 bob a week, decided there were better jobs, and it was up to me to get one.

I turned in at the newsagent's. 'Hope you've managed to pick out one or two winners,' one of the lads said. It was always assumed you'd 'have a tanner on' when you started working.

I bought a copy of the *Nottingham Evening News* and went home. The cricket scores were read and digested and then I turned to the 'situations vacant' columns. Mam said, 'I'm glad to see you're looking for another job because it's nothing but all that water slopping about that's given you your throat.' 'Yes, Mam,' I said and scoured the advertisements with growing desperation. And then I read: 'Smart boy wanted for Lace Manufacturer's office.'

'Here,' I said, 'what about this?' And handed the paper to my mother.

She read it carefully and then looked at me over the top of her glasses. 'They don't always pay good wages in offices,' she said.

'Go on, lad, have a shot,' said my father; 'you've nothing to lose.'

My mother, ever practical, got out writing paper and envelope and set them down in front of me. 'Right, that's it then. And do your best handwriting. Not that scrawl I've seen you do.'

Carefully the letter was composed, written out in rough and then copied out in as fair a hand as I could manage. Mam read it with great care, nodded approval and said 'Right, I've got a three-ha'penny stamp in my purse. Seal up the envelope and I'll take it down to the letterbox. And you'd best gargle and get off to bed. We don't want you laid up for Monday.'

So bed it was. And it was typical of her. My wage might be only 12 shillings a week (less train fares) but I owed it to my boss to be at work if at all possible. In our house scrounging – on whatever pretext – was out of the question. Duty was the guiding light and you'd better be punctual into the bargain.

It was early the following week, while I was struggling with the usual mountain of bottles and wondering how I should get through the day, that one of the girls from the office came across the cobbled yard and told the foreman I was wanted on the telephone. My heart missed a few beats. Wanted on the phone? That could only mean something terrible. Somebody at home had dropped dead, the house was on fire, or my young sister had been run over. And – added obstacle – I had never used a phone.

I was in such a bewildered panic that the foreman said, 'Go on, lad, go and see what it is. You're mostly as red as a beetroot but you look as if you've seen a ghost this time'.

Five minutes later I had taken the call and that was a major stride forward but, more importantly, the voice on the line had asked me to go to the other end of the town to be interviewed. Not that anything would be settled even then, the voice had been quick to tell me, I was just one of a number of lads to be seen.

My present boss was sitting there while I answered the phone. He didn't look very happy about the situation, and when I asked him if I could leave a bit earlier that evening he barked 'Yes!' Just that one word, but enough to make me think he'd probably sack me for even daring to apply for another job.

I stammered out my thanks and went back to my bottles.

The foreman, who was a kindly man and a Salvationist, came over to me. 'Everything all right, son? No trouble or anything, is there?'

'No, sir.' I said. There was no need to call him 'sir'. I had never done so before but I was so overwhelmed by what had happened.

The old foreman smiled, nodded and merely said, 'Right, get on with your work then.'

I got on with my work for the rest of the day, and wondered if I would be able to find my way to Canal Street at the other side of the town. That was one worry; the other was that I had spent twopence on a bar of chocolate on my way to work that morning and, consequently, had no money.

Fortunately, there was Arthur. He was the assistant foreman, easily approachable and, he seemed to me, very mature. At lunchtime I asked him if he could tell me how to get to Canal Street. And could he lend me the bus fare until tomorrow. 'No bother at all, Mark,' he said, 'and the best of luck.'

I took off my clogs and rubber apron and hung them in the shed just inside the big green gates. Still in overalls and clutching the little case I carried my lunch in I caught the bus as Arthur had directed. How marvellous, I thought, to know the city so well.

My main concern as I got off the bus was whether I looked smart enough and I wondered if I ought to take off my overalls. But I decided against it. 'So long as you're clean,' my mother was fond of saying. 'Always look as if you belong to somebody.' Well, I'd had a wash and combed my hair and I pulled down my jacket as I approached the imposing entrance. *Office*, directed a large pointing finger painted on the wall above the doorway. I rang the bell at the side of the enquiries window and waited.

Suddenly the frosted glass window shot up, a large round face appeared and I was told to enter a door at right angles to the window.

'Whenever you're faced with anything important take a few deep breaths,' I had heard my father say, and I thought that was what I should be doing. But I always seemed to remember those helpful bits of advice too late, and I suddenly found myself sitting in a wooden armchair, case on the floor beside me, and looking at the man who had bidden me enter. He was perched on a high stool looking down at me, eyes like two shiny currants in his podgy face. He had a list in his hand and glanced at it from time to time as he began to ask questions.

'Are you a good timekeeper?'

'Yes, sir, I am'.

'Aye, well you live a fair distance away and you'd have to be here at nine o'clock sharp.'

I knew that would be no problem because I had to be at my present job at eight.

'And we don't knock off until half-past five. Think you can cope with that?'

Not half, I would have liked to have said; we don't finish until six where I'm working now. But I simply said I was sure I could manage.

'How about illnesses? Are you often away from work?'

'I keep very well, sir.'

'Never been in trouble, have you? With the police, I mean'.

'No, sir.'

'Good. Well, you look clean enough. Have you got a respectable suit?'

'Yes, sir,' I said. I knew my mother would let me wear my Sunday best and perhaps I could save a bit towards a new one.

And then, seemingly accidentally, a coin dropped on to the floor. Almost as a reflex I was out of my chair and after it.

'Thank you,' said Mr Preston as I handed it back to him and there was the faintest of smiles on his face. That was the moment, I think, when he decided to give me the job. But my heart sank into my boots when he said, 'Well now, I've a few more lads to see. I shall let you know in due course.' And, as I was

Steam train at Nottingham Victoria. A twice-a-day journey was my schedule for many years. While a juvenile my season ticket cost 12s 2d per month.

leaving him he said, 'By the way, do you know this boy? He must live somewhere close to you.' He had a letter in his hand and he mentioned the name of a lad who had been in my class at school. That cast a spell of deep gloom but I tried not to show it as I said goodnight. And I remembered to say thank you. I could picture my mother as I told her what had happened. She would listen intently and then say, 'I hope you remembered to say thank you.'

I spent the remaining three-halfpence of Arthur's loan on a bus ride to Victoria Station and managed to catch my usual train home.

'Well,' said my dad, 'you've tried, that's the main thing.'

I agreed, and kept silent about the application that had been made by the lad who had been in the same class.

It was a couple of days later that I had a postcard from Mr Preston asking me to go and see him again; 'for a final interview' it read in what my mother called 'this beautiful writing'.

This time I was able to treat myself to a chocolate bar and still have a shilling in my pocket for the necessary bus fare. 'I shall expect some change, mind,' said my mother. This time I had to go to work in my best suit, which meant being careful during the day to avoid the inevitable water that was splashed around the bottling plant.

'And try to give your boots a bit of a rub before you go to your interview.' Mam put a square of cloth in the case, along with my sandwiches. 'Try and look smart whether you get the job or not. And hold your shoulders back.'

It was ever the same. There was always a long list of instructions and mostly they were accompanied by a bit of action. All good sound stuff, no doubt, but you had to be on your guard. 'Hold your shoulders back' was the cue for a thump to let you know where Mam thought the hump might be developing; 'Pull down your jacket' – and before you knew what was happening the bottom edge of the garment was yanked down towards the buttocks; 'Keep your tie straight' – and the job was done for you with a consequent constriction of the neck that threatened to interfere with the blood supply.

But I did remember to rub my boots.

I was glad I had gone in my best suit because Mr Preston said, 'I suppose that's the suit you'll be wearing if I give you the job?'

Chapter One

'Yes, sir.'

'Right. Now sit down there. I shall be back in a minute.'

I looked around. The office was beautifully panelled in a deep red wood; there was a large safe at one end and there was a fixed desk that ran the entire length of the room on the street side. There were drawer sections in the desk and spaces for two stools. One of the stools and the chair I was sitting in were to polish the seats of a good many pairs of my trousers over the next 20 years. But for the moment I simply sat, tense and wondering what the next move might be. On the desk was an old-fashioned telephone, with the part you spoke into at the top of a metal stick and the earpiece suspended at the side on a bracket. What would I do if it rang, I wondered anxiously. It was the prospect of that more than anything else that worried me as I sat there.

Then there were footsteps and voices and Mr Preston appeared, accompanied by a jolly-looking woman wearing a black overall.

'This,' said Mr Preston, arm pointing towards me, 'is Mark. And this, Mark, is Miss Skeet.'

'Well, and how do you do, young man?'

We shook hands and before I could say anything Mr Preston said, 'Now, do you think we might find room for him?'

Miss Skeet eyed me keenly. 'So long as he does as he's told I think he might do.'

'Right,' Mr Preston said. Miss Skeet, smiling, turned on her heel and went.

'I've decided to give you the job,' he went on, 'and before you go I think I might have a word with your old boss and ask him if he'll let you go without a week's notice so that you can start here next Monday.'

'Tell him to come and see me when he gets to work tomorrow,' was the message relayed by Mr Preston, and, on the following morning, convinced that I was going to receive a severe ticking-off, I mounted the dark wooden stairs to the office that looked out over the bottling plant. But I needn't have worried. The boss, who was usually gruff and a bit frightening, was pleasant enough and even managed a weak smile as he handed me my cards stamped up to date. 'Best of luck, lad,' he said.

'Whatever you do, don't forget to thank him,' my mother had instructed before I left home. And, as I was scuttling down the entry to make sure I caught my train, she shouted after me: 'Now, don't forget! Say thank you!'

So it came out pat as I was handed my cards. But by then the boss had his head bent over a pile of papers and whether he heard me or not I'll never know. Maybe he was just in a hurry to clear his desk and – as Arthur was fond of saying – 'get his fat arse on one of his horses'.

I said my cheerios that evening to the lads I had worked with over the past few months, pocketed my money and caught the train home, sharing a compartment with the lad who had told me about the vacancy at the bottling plant in the first place. He didn't seem too pleased when he knew I should be able to catch a later train from the following Monday.

'How much are they going to pay you, then?' he asked.

'Twelve and a tanner,' I said. That was something mother and father wouldn't have approved of, telling someone how much I was to be paid. 'Keep your own counsel,' my dad always said. But the temptation to impart the information was just too strong.

'Well, bloody 'ell,' said my companion. 'Working less hours and getting a tanner more. Lucky sod.'

Chapter Two

'ARE you the new office boy?' asked Bill Dolman the following Monday morning. 'Yes,' I said. Bill grinned and displayed his broken black teeth. And black is precisely what I mean. They were as black as the clumping, clanking lace machines I was seeing for the first time. It has been said more than once that it is a source of wonder that something so fine and delicate as lace and net can be made by such massive pieces of machinery. It is almost as if a battleship had to be used to make a few ripples on a pond.

I had left home that morning in my best suit, new shirt and tie, and wearing boots polished to a state that would have done credit to a guardsman. It was another of my mother's pieces of advice to live by that you always wore highly polished footwear. She led by example. She might be going no farther than the corner shop but she was neat and tidy and her shoes shone.

'Let yourself go,' she used to say, 'and you're on the downward path. There's plenty of slovenliness about without adding to it.' That was the measure of her pride and discipline; and she needed plenty of one to keep up the other on the pittance the state paid to an out-of-work miner in the grim 1930s.

'When you come on Monday morning,' Mr Preston had said to me, 'use the employees' entrance. Sit in the room behind the office and wait for me.' I did as I was told, arriving at about a quarter to nine and perching myself on a stool, trying to appear to the old lady busying about the place with duster, brush and dustpan as though this was something I did every day.

She barely paused in her work, apart from a cursory glance that took in me and my case. 'Waiting for Jack, are you?'

'Mr Preston,' I said.

'Ah well, he's Jack to most of us. We've known him a long time, you see.' She went on with her sweeping and dusting. 'You're not very old, are you?'

'I'm 14,' I said.

'Lord, I wish I were. My name's Mrs Mallison. I've got a grandson owder than you.'

She grabbed a mop and started to clean a bit of lino outside one of the office doors. 'This is Jack's office,' she said. 'He's very particular, you know. Likes things nice. Have to be ever so careful with the brasses. Oh, you'll be all right. Keep out o' mischief and do as he tells you.' It could have been my mother talking.

When Mrs Mallison went to fetch fresh water I looked around the long room. There were scores of bundles of lace and net stacked in wooden racks and one single dim electric light was the only illumination. The muffled sound of machinery came from somewhere beyond the whitewashed walls and now and then there was the sound of women's voices, the conversation broken from time to time by laughter. And then Mrs Mallison reappeared. 'Mr Preston has just come into t'yard in his car,' she said. It was as though, having him near in person, the familiar 'Jack' was dropped in favour of the more formal 'Mr Preston'.

A car door slammed and a second or two later Mr Preston arrived. 'Morning, Jack,' Mrs Mallison said, familiarity returning.

'Morning.' And then, seeing me: 'Now then, young man, come along.'

I went with him into the general office and watched him open the large green safe. Packed inside were about two dozen books. Half of them were heavy leather-bound ledgers standing upright; smaller account books were piled on top of them.

'These are the books you will be using every day and I want you to be very careful with your figures.' The smaller books he placed on top of the safe; four or five of the larger ones on a table standing against the back wall of the office.

'I like to see figures done neatly,' he went on, 'and I want you to take care with your writing. I put a new Golden Shoulder nib in your pen last Friday.

Chapter Two

Don't put too much ink on it until you get used to it. Now, enter these tickets. I'll do a couple for you and then you'll see how it's done.'

Mr Preston opened one of the large books on the desk. 'Get sat on your stool,' he said, 'and watch me.' I watched as he took the top two off a pile of tickets. Each ticket stated the width, type and quality of a piece – or web – of lace, together with a serial number, which machine it was made on and the name of the man responsible. But, equally important, the number of faults in the piece and how much it had cost to mend.

I watched as the practised hand filled in the details. If I had sat on the stool for ever I could not have matched the handwriting, and my mind went back to my mother's comments when she saw the postcard that had arrived at our house summoning me for the interview. I was in a state of nervous tension when the pen was handed to me with the instruction to carry on with the rest of the tickets.

Mr Preston stood by my side as I made my first entries. When I had written the details from a couple of tickets I paused, ostensibly to dip my pen in the inkwell at the top of the desk, but really it was to take a deep breath and flex my fingers. At the same time I stole a glance at the boss's face. It was impassive but I sensed he must have been disappointed with my first effort. My handwriting looked immature and ill-formed following as it did his ornate flourishes. But he merely said 'Right, make it as neat as you can. And go carefully.'

With that he disappeared into his own office. I had the distinct feeling that he might be wishing he had given me a handwriting test before setting me on. And he must have wondered if he might have been happier if he had given one of the other applicants the job. He had told me he'd had letters from 28 lads. I felt, as I sat there that sunny Monday morning, that I might not have been the best of the bunch. But it was so pleasant to be sitting there after the sweat and grind of the bottling plant that I determined to make each entry a bit better than the last, and my reward was when Miss Skeet, entering the office so quietly I hadn't heard her, stood at my side, peering at my entries and said 'Very nice, Mark, very nice.'

She then went into Mr Preston's office and I heard her say 'Good morning, Jack, nice mornin'. Now I've just been looking at young Mark's cottons an' he's entered 'em very neat I think.'

'Aye,' I heard Mr Preston say, 'they teach 'em a different style than they did when I was at school.'

I had obviously made a better impression on Miss Skeet than on the boss. I could tell from his tone that he was prepared to tolerate what for him was the best of a bad job. But I couldn't have matched his convoluted style if I had sat over one entry an entire day.

And then my heart missed a few beats. 'An' now then, Jack, I'm goin' to suggest he comes and gives me a hand in the mending room. He'd better get some idea of what we have to do.'

The mending room was the place from where the laughter had come when I'd been sitting behind the offices waiting for Mr Preston to arrive. Now Miss Skeet was proposing that I should go into the place.

A moment later and Mr Preston had walked into the office and said 'Mark, I want you to go with Bess and give her a hand.' I would have liked to have said 'But I thought I was supposed to work in the office.' In fact, all I said was 'Right, sir,' and laid down my pen.

'Come along,' said Miss Skeet, who had bustled to the door leading into the piece room. I slid off my stool and, heart beating madly, accompanied her.

As we stood outside the mending room door she said 'Oh, by the way, call me Bess, not Miss Skeet. Everybody calls me Bess. But that doesn't mean I'm soft with 'em. No, my word, not at all, not at all. And it was my idea you should come into this room and help me. That way, you see, you'll learn a bit o' something about the trade. It's no good sittin' on that there stool enterin' all them tickets and things and not knowin' what it's all about. Is it now?'

'No, Bess,' I said.

She turned and bustled on and I followed her. There, in a long room, with windows along one side looking out on to the works yard, sat maybe a dozen girls, every one of them wearing a black overall and sitting on a low stool. Each of the girls was surrounded by – perhaps it would be more accurate to say partially enveloped by – a mound of white lace.

When I entered the room I heard one voice above the rest. It was meant to be a stage whisper I suppose. 'Here he is then,' it said. There was muffled giggling. Bess was obviously expecting some reaction.

Chapter Two

'Get on with your work,' she commanded. 'There's no time to sit gawpin' around you.' When she spoke all the heads bent over and the mending was resumed. But there was still some subdued laughter. I felt acutely embarrassed and wished I was anywhere but there.

But Bess was talking, and as she did so she grabbed my arm and took me over to the nearest girl. 'Now, watch carefully. This girl is puttin' a stitch in.' I watched as the girl dexterously plied her needle and within a few seconds the break in the lace was no longer discernible. Bess led me over to another girl.

'Now this girl is mending a bodge.' I looked and saw a messy break in the piece of lace the girl had spread tight over her knee. Threads were hanging down and there was a dirty area surrounding the place. 'Now, see what she does. She'll cut off the threads she can't work back into the net and put new threads in.' I watched, admiring the speed and expertise of the girl. Bess walked away to answer a question another girl was putting to her. As she did so the girl I was watching looked over her shoulder at me and gave me an enormous wink. 'Hello… Mark.' It was said just loud enough for one or two of the others to hear. There was another burst of muffled giggling and Bess turned quickly.

'I've warned some of you lot. An' I shan't do it again. You'll be signin'-on before you're much older if you're not careful.'

I stood trying to watch, and with cheeks burning like fires. The girl was now back at her skilful work; only by her gently shaking shoulders did I know she was still enjoying life at my expense.

Bess came over. 'Now then, I want you to help me count a few pieces. You'll soon see what it's all about.' She led the way to the far end of the room towards a large black board, standing on two iron stanchions and placed at an angle so that when a piece of lace was draped over it was possible, by walking up and down the full length of the board, to see at once any faults in the making.

'Now, this is what we 'ave to do to price the work, see. You look for any faults, count how many there are and what sort, and then at the end you've a good idea how long it should take a girl to mend. Do you understand, dear?' She had a voice, not particularly loud, but clear, and in the silence of the room it echoed. She was very slightly deaf, but I wasn't, and from somewhere in the distance came the parrot-cry, very low, but distinct: 'Do you understand, dear?' Low laughter swiftly went round the girls sitting mending.

I was glad when that first teaching session was over and I could escape to the peace and silence of the office.

'Well, and how did you get on with Bess, lad?' asked Mr Preston.

'Very well, sir,' I lied.

'Lasses laugh at you?'

'Just a bit, sir.'

'Aye, I thought they might. But there's not a deal of harm in 'em. Like a bit o' fun, though,' and he laughed, his eyes almost disappearing in his podgy cheeks.

'Oh, there's one more thing I want to tell you. Don't call me "sir". I don't mind a bit of respect from a young chap but I don't expect you to call me "sir". But, at the same time, I don't expect you to call me "Jack". Most o' the folk in the factory do because they've known me a long time. I should like you to say "Mr Preston".'

'Right,' I said and then listened for the first time – but certainly not the last – to how he had started life in the factory as a shop lad fetching 'three ha'porth o' milk and a couple o' bacon sandwiches for first one and then the other and after that moving on to be a threader-lad, brass-bobbin winder and then, after the army, into the office until I became manager.'

Now here was a man my father would have admired. 'Never be frightened of hard work,' my dad had said umpteen times, 'and then you'll get on'.

Well, here was a man who had got on right enough and for a day or two I was suitable awed.

But what had happened to the previous office boy, I wanted to ask. Yet there was no time. He was in full flight again but this time about Bess. 'One o' the best in the trade,' he said. 'She comes from the west of England. You can probably tell that by the way she talks.'

She spoke with a soft burr and pronounced words somewhat differently to the way we did in Nottinghamshire but I had no idea which part of the country she came from.

'Aye,' Mr Preston continued, 'there were a lot of them who came up from Chard or thereabouts. We've a few of them in the factory. And Bess was one.

A good friend of mine. If you treat her right she'll teach you plenty.'

When I returned to my desk I found a new interest in entering the work tickets and looking carefully at the assessments of the faults.

It was later in the morning that Bess came through the general office where I sat and straight into Mr Preston's inner sanctum. There was some low muttering and then I heard her say 'Oh yes, he seemed to take an interest. Of course, you never can tell in one so young.'

On her way back to the mending room she stopped by my side. 'Jack wanted to know how you'd gone on. I told him I thought you might be all right.' She smiled, patted me on the back, and went on her way.

'Thank you,' I said to her disappearing back and felt a good deal more content.

My first few lunches were taken in the stock room – by order!

I recall well enough that my lunch that first day was cheese and tomato sandwiches, a piece of homemade seed cake and a drink of water. There was no canteen in the place and when lunchtime came Mr Preston told me to take my case out into the dimly lit piece room and eat my sandwiches there. 'I don't want the office opened up until I get back. Understand?'

And so my first lunch was eaten in lonely isolation. As I munched away I could hear the chattering of the girls as they went in and out of the mending room, and so that they wouldn't see me I piled a few bundles of lace on to the long counter and set out my lunch behind the barricade. It seemed a bit daft to have to sit out there when there was a reasonably comfortable wooden armchair in the general office. Well, maybe in a day or two I would chance it. After all, the office key was hanging inside the little wardrobe standing next to the washbasin where I'd been told I could hang my clothes. And that was how it worked out. For the first few days I waited until Mr Preston had gone home and then I sneaked into the office, taking care to be out again and with the key hanging in the appropriate place, until I heard him coming in the back way. As he appeared up the steps I would be fumbling with the key in the lock. That seemed to impress him; sitting there waiting for the sound of his footsteps and them jumping up to make sure the office was open for him to stride through unimpeded. Then came the reward. 'Now then, Mark, you can stay in the office at lunchtime if you like and eat your sandwiches there.'

'Thank you,' I said and tried to make it sound that I'd been accorded a great privilege.

So, day in and day out, I caught my train to work and walked at a fair speed through Nottingham so that I should be at the office at nine o'clock sharp. There was the odd occasion when the train was a bit late, causing me to worry that I might be given a roasting. On those days – and there was not much that upset the old LNER schedule – I would set off like a hare, be one of the first through the ticket barrier, and scoot hell for leather through the busy city.

And I was not the only one to do so. To arrive late at some of the big works meant there was a good chance of being locked out and losing money. More than once I'd heard it said: 'If you're late at our place they stop you a quarter of an hour.' I could hardly see that happening at Peggoty's but 'you never know who might report you,' said my mother. So, on the odd occasions when something went wrong I ran – and damned hard.

Very soon I had settled into the daily routine. It started by my having a word or two with Mrs Mallison and, when she went about her business, a surreptitious read of *The Morning Post*, taking care to fold it into its original creases before the boss arrived. I remember being puzzled by the city pages. They didn't appear in the paper we had at home and I wondered what they were all about. But there were some entertaining cricket reports and I was always anxious to know how Notts had fared, and in particular Joe Hardstaff, then just setting out on his illustrious career. Voce and Larwood were established players, gods who walked on hallowed turf on the other side of the Trent.

Trent Bridge, scene of much enjoyment over many years.

What a marvellous way to earn a living, I thought, as I sat on my office stool through the dying days of that first summer at Peggoty's, being able to play cricket on the famous Trent Bridge ground. The memory of the first match I'd seen there still remained fresh and exciting. It was on a Saturday and Nottinghamshire were playing Worcestershire. The ground, the pavilion, the scoreboards – they had all been described to me by my father. Up to that Saturday the only games I had seen had been on the local parks; Trent Bridge lived up to all that I had been told about it.

We sat at the opposite end of the ground to the pavilion. In the far left-hand corner from us, under the scoreboard, there was an enormous roller and sitting beside it an old man. Dad's voice dropped to a reverential whisper as he said: 'That is Walter Marshall. He's the groundsman here. One of the finest in the country. Doesn't matter how good a cricketer you are, you've got to have a true wicket to play on. An' old Walter makes sure Trent Bridge is kept in tip-top condition.' It was obviously a tremendous responsibility to look after such a playing piece; I was suitably impressed. Dad went on: 'Larwood's got a lot to thank him for and so has Bill Voce.'

'What about the batsmen?' I asked.

'Aye, them an' all,' he said.

I can't remember in detail what happened that day but I do recall C.F. Walters opening for Worcestershire and delighting the crowd with some majestic batting. Yes, I thought, it must be wonderful to get your living playing cricket. But on Monday it was back to the stern reality of Peggoty's and lace.

It was surprising how quickly dashing around the factory on this errand or that, counting the pieces of lace and net with old Bess Skeet, and learning not to take too much notice of what was said by the menders, seemed to become part and parcel of the rapidly-passing days.

It was an odd set-up, though, just Mr Preston and me to do the office work, and one day I plucked up enough courage to ask Bess who had been there before me. 'Oh, old Mr Skelhorn,' she said. 'An' from what I've heard he be hoping to come back. Mind you, I can't see that 'appening. Broke 'is leg a month or two back and Jack 'ad to take over the runnin'.'

'Oh, I see,' I said.

I began to worry in case Mr Skelhorn came back and I should be given the

Chapter Two

sack. For the rest of the week I found it difficult to think about much else, and I visualised that one Saturday morning just before we knocked off I should be told I wasn't really suitable and that my packet contained a week's money in lieu of notice. But surely Mr Preston wouldn't do that, I told myself, not after he'd interviewed me and sent me to the factory doctor and made his entry in the works register.

It was no good: I'd have to say something. But old Bess must have mentioned it one day when she was talking to Mr Preston. I remember I'd carefully folded *The Morning Post* and put it away, having for once looked at the cricket scores without enthusiasm, when the boss said: 'Now, young man, I reckon you've been asking Bess what the position was before you came here. I think she told you Mr Skelhorn was the manager. Well, that's quite right, he was. But he had an accident and broke his leg. And seeing he's well over 70 he's decided to retire. So, as long as you work well there's no need to worry. Is that clear?'

'Yes, Mr Preston.'

He started to walk back to his own office but stopped suddenly and turned. 'Oh, and I've decided to raise your wages. From today you'll be getting 16 shillings a week.'

I simply could not believe it. Sixteen shillings a week. A rise of three-and-sixpence and I had been there only a month. When I caught the train that night it seemed to take hours for it to leave the station and days for it to get me home. Clutching my little attaché case I ran as hard as I could to impart the good news and put my pay packet on the table.

My mother and father were delighted. 'That's what comes of trying hard,' Mam said, and my dinner tasted extra good.

It had nagged me a bit, this question of wages, ever since I'd run into Rex MacDermott a week or two before. He had started work in the local Co-op as a flour lad and was as proud as a peacock as he told me about his prospects. 'There aren't many jobs, y'know,' he said, 'where you can say what wages you'll be getting when you're 21. I shall be earning three pounds seven-and-six a week.' His future, it seemed to me, was really settled and there was a twinge of envy as I thought about my 12-and-six, with little idea of what my wage might eventually be.

But 16 bob at 14 years of age! That wasn't such a bad start.

Yet the heady delight was short-lived. A few days later, when I walked in from work, it was obvious there was an air of gloom about the house. I could sense it although Mam was trying her best to be cheerful. 'What's up?' I asked.

I looked hard at her face and knew there had been tears.

'Why, you get a rise and your dad's money's knocked down.'

And that is what had happened. Dad was on the Means Test and there was a declared amount allowed to come into the house by the way of dole and earnings. Dad's money amounted to a few shillings; I can't remember exactly how much but it couldn't have been more than 30 bob to keep the four of us. When I started to work the overall amount was increased by my wages of 12-and-sixpence and for a few weeks my mother, as thrifty as they came, must have thought she was in clover. The clover would have been even more lush if she could have had the extra three-and-sixpence. But that wasn't to be. The rise in my wages was knocked off my dad's money.

Sitting there eating my meal I felt, perhaps for the first time, a sense of real bitterness about the injustice of the system that allowed a miner who had contracted nystagmus and was declared unfit to work at the coalface to be kept to the level of grinding poverty. It was to be years before he found regular work and his wounded pride was healed.

But youth is seldom down for long and life at Peggoty's went on.

Chapter Three

I T WAS a matter of some concern to my mother that I had to walk through a notorious part of Nottingham to get to work. I remember that when I came home from my interview and explained the location of the factory, Mam's consternation was obvious. 'That's a rum area,' she said. 'Aye,' my dad chipped in, 'bobbies have to go about in twos.'

Far from feeling scared, the idea of going by Broad Marsh and down Sussex Street appealed to me. I recall vividly my first Monday morning. At a quarter to eight (I'd insisted on going early that first day) the neighbourhood was a hive of activity, with a steady stream of workers hurrying towards Boots, then one of the great industrial concerns of the city.

Sussex Street was a bewitching thoroughfare and somebody at Peggoty's told me there had been a time when there were 14 pubs from the eastern end of the street to the top of Drury Hill. I never knew whether that was fact or fiction but I could well imagine it to be fact. The distance in question couldn't have been much more than a quarter of a mile. There were a few pubs when I first knew the area, and the street itself was so narrow that a hop, step and jump would have taken you from one side to the other. Houses, dozens of them, propped each other up and one wondered how the occupants survived. It was said the places were so stinkingly hot in summer that the tenants would sit outside until the early hours of the morning, smoking and gossiping because it was impossible to sleep inside.

There were shops in abundance among the houses and one I got to know well was Marriott's, almost on the corner of Sussex Street and Canal Street. Old man Marriott was a newsagent; even on a bright day the interior of his shop was never really light. Standing at the counter waiting to be served you were aware of his approach well before you could see him as he shuffled over the stone floor. He was a large man, of few words. When I could afford it I spent a morning penny on the *Daily Mail*, buying my first copy when there was a story of Sapper's being serialised. After that initial purchase it became vitally important to follow the adventures of Jim Maitland. The stories of Sapper were special and I had devoured his Bulldog Drummond tales with enormous relish, paying twopence a week membership to a local library and reaching the end of each book with sadness because I knew it would be some time before the next was published.

Old Mr Skelhorn had been a good customer at the corner shop. He had, apparently, always been a keen sportsman, passionately interested in cricket, cycling and boxing. And he was an authority on cage birds. Marriott delivered a number of weeklies to the office for him so that he could keep abreast of events, and when Jack Preston was sure his old boss wouldn't be coming back to work he instructed me to go across to the newsagent's to cancel a long-standing order.

Mr Marriott grunted. 'So the old lad is retiring, eh?' He grunted again. 'Pity that, pity. A real break with the past. Known him some years. Grand old fella. Tough as a walnut and about as wrinkled. I shall miss him. Wonder who'll go first, him or me, eh? Could be me. He had no more meat on him than a fourpenny rabbit.' He shuffled out of the shop and through to the back of the premises.

Intermingled with the pubs and houses of Sussex Street two neighbouring shops were known to the scores of factory workers. One was a place run by a tiny wizened old woman who seemed to be forever on the run. She would take your order while still moving, trot around the shop, sometimes nip into her kitchen if the purchase was not immediately to hand, and still be jigging about while she waited for your money. It always struck me that the place was none too hygienic, but that never seemed to be a major worry to those who found the shop convenient. There was a constant procession for a ha'porth of milk, a couple of custards or a bar of chocolate. What sort of a

Drury Hill, a
place of
enchantment.

backyard had a place like that, I wondered. Was there one? Or was the front entrance the only means of access? I suppose there must have been a way in at the back but there were so many buildings about that none of them seemed to have space enough for all the amenities.

Perhaps nowhere had a stronger place in the affection of the locals than the shop next door – Owd Wardy's the barber's. 'George Ward' proclaimed the fancy painted notice on the wall above the door, but the place was known to all and sundry as Owd Wardy's. A copper or two for a haircut and, if you wanted a shave as well, the combined operation would be carried out for sixpence. You had to time your visit or you could be there for an hour, so busy did the place become. And some of the twisthands from Peggoty's were not above taking your place in the queue. 'Can't be long. I've got a piece coming off in 20 minutes. Time's money and I don't want my butty shouting the odds 'cos there's a machine standing.'

But I for one was never in any hurry to get out of Owd Wardy's because it was a fascinating place and a gathering point for some of the characters in the area. Ribald humour abounded (how could it be otherwise when French letters were laid out in the window priced at twopence each and for extra strength fourpence?) and it was not possible to sit there long without adding to one's knowledge of the rougher side of life.

Close by George Ward's saloon (it deserved the title of saloon, especially first thing on a Saturday morning, when the place was swept and bright and the brass fittings and glass advertisements sparkled) was a wide entry to a printing works where Peggoty's bought their envelopes and wage packets. The packets were minute affairs but big enough to hold the modest sums that were put into them. It was on this site, incidentally, that John Player, in 1877, had his first tobacco factory.

'When you've taken that order to the printer's you might as well get the insurance stamps from Middle Pavement post office.' That instruction was like offering an invitation to dip into a bag of jewels. It meant the opportunity to dawdle up Drury Hill and, later, dawdle down again. There was usually a queue in the post office and if there wasn't I could invent one. Surely I wouldn't be missed for 10 minutes.

Drury Hill was the city's El Dorado, an enchanting thoroughfare, from the

Sussex Street, a famously narrow thoroughfare with enticing shops.

plumbing establishment of Henry Ball and Company at the bottom, to the busy hand-written poster shop at the top. Peggoty's plumbing requirements (and there always seemed to be something amiss) were dealt with by Henry Ball and Company, as like as not by old Henry himself. He was actively engaged in the business until a very advanced age and one bright memory I have is of him cycling down Sussex Street to Peggoty's, waistcoat flapping in the morning breeze, and then watching him climb the four-storey fire escape to put a pane of glass in the top-most door. His son Walter, no spring chicken himself, said of him: 'Silly owd bugger. One slip and a puff o' wind and he could have been in t'canal.' But old Henry was never one to shirk work or the chance to earn a few bob.

On both sides of Drury Hill were antique shops, with knick-knacks littered among pieces of china, glass and pottery that, if offered for sale today, would doubtless be worth a packet. But there wasn't the popular interest then in antiques. One day Jack Preston gave me an envelope to take to one of the dealers. 'No need to wait for an answer,' he said. 'Just go into the shop and say I've sent it.' He must have seen my curiosity. 'The chap who owns the shop is a bit down on his luck. He was telling me the other day he hadn't had a sale for the best part of a week. I've decided I ought to treat him. I'm sending him a ticket for the regimental dinner. He was in France with me during the war.'

Some of the antique shops had books for sale, but when it came to books none of them could compare with Welton's. Here, indeed, was delight; but when I told my mother and father about the place they exchanged looks that seemed a bit furtive, I thought, and when Dad was on his own I asked him if he knew the shop. 'Yes,' he said, 'it's well known. Old man Welton is a very advanced thinker and sends out some odd books and catalogues. He lectures all over the place. Or did. Matter of fact I think he's dead.' That seemed a bit of a jumble and I didn't pursue it. But I looked with even greater interest the next time I went by.

There was nothing like today's variety of bright book jackets then. Most seemed a bit dull, but I did spot one in a garish green, over-printed with a heavily-made bearded gentleman standing in the attitude of a lecturer beside a stand on which stood a flourishing plant. This, I assumed, would be Mr Welton. And, perusing the contents of the window closely, there did seem to be a number of books on sex. But to a 14-year-old boy they did little more than implant a mild curiosity. The brightest of all the display was a book on cricket by Jack Hobbs. Time after time I went to look and wondered if I could afford the half-crown for it. But out of a bob a week spending money that would have meant saving up. I did once think it might be worthwhile asking the lady who I'd seen in the shop from time to time if she would put it aside for me, but more pressing matters chased the idea away. The lady, I was told, was Mr Welton's daughter. Did she, so prim and neat – and invariably the wearer of a large flowered hat – ever hear the famous lectures or read the books offered for sale in the intriguing window?

Drury Hill forked left at the far end of Sussex Street; straight ahead were the steps of Middle Hill. Two sets of steps there were, with a few yards of walking between them, and on this nearly level stretch stood two houses. They are gone now, but they were captured for ever on film when D.H. Lawrence's *Sons and Lovers* was made. One of the interiors was used and the

Middle Hill – not the place it was when our safecracker had his business there.

mock-up fireplace that was part of the set was stored until wanted in the yard of Henry Ball and Company; and it was around this area that early one morning, while most of the city slept, actors did their stuff in a machine-made snowstorm.

Just beyond the Middle Hill houses a locksmith had his premises and there was a never-to-be-forgotten day when I had to go and ask the small and very polite bald-headed craftsman if he could come straightaway to Peggoty's to open the general office safe. Jack Preston had lost the keys and was getting frantic at the possibility of not being able to get at the money to pay the weekly wages. His first reaction was to walk up and down the office wringing his hands and saying: 'What the hell am I going to do, Mark? What the hell am I going to do?'

The unflappable locksmith calmly surveyed the safe and the lock, carefully spread his tools on the floor and, after working dexterously on his knees for about five minutes, there were a few clicks and the heavy doors were swung open. All was once again serene. The little man packed up his tools, carefully

Homeward bound from the Lace Market's Stoney Street about 100 years ago.

Chapter Three

folded and pocketed the five-pound note Jack Preston insisted upon giving
him and went out humming, the tenor of his life scarcely disturbed, but
leaving a young lad gaping in admiration.

Drury Hill and Middle Hill were two famous thoroughfares. There was a
third, and after dark it was a forbidding place to go. Garner's Hill ran for a
little distance under the railway connecting the east side of the city to
Nottingham Victoria. Walk under there alone and your echoing footsteps
made it difficult to restrain the impulse to run. But you had to be in pretty
good nick to make any speed, for beyond the bit under the railway you were
faced with more than 30 steps (not altogether, but in a series, with steep
walking in between) before you arrived on High Pavement.

Surfacing there gave little cause for concern, for a few yards away was a
police station, and beyond, the old Shire Hall and the former county jail. But
it was, for all that, pretty eerie even there after dark, under the shadow of the
famous church of St Mary's, bordered by the quiet streets of the city's Lace
Market. St Mary's Gate and Stoney Street were hives of commercial activity
during the day but once evening came and the hundreds of workers had gone
home, it was all silence and ghostliness between the tall and ancient buildings.

Chapter Four

IT WAS the custom at Peggoty's to have a works outing each summer and one day Bess said to me: 'I shall 'ave to 'ave a word with Jack about the outing for next year.'

'But it's only November,' I said.

She laughed. 'That's as maybe, but you 'ave to think about such things early. As soon as Christmas is over we've got to give a thought or two to where we might go. An' I like to remind Jack in good time so that 'e can think about it.'

All was obviously done to a pattern, following a routine that had been tried and tested. My first Christmas at the firm came and went (there had been a 'seasonal' five shillings in my pay packet) and early in January a notice was pinned on the side of the huge old grandfather-type clock that stood in the ground floor machine shop.

Some days later Jack Preston said: 'I've had a word with one or two folks, Mark, and it seems there could be a bit of support for a trip to Liverpool. Ever been to Liverpool?'

'No, I haven't,' I said.

'Place well worth visiting. Anyhow, let's leave the notice up for a bit and see how it goes.'

I'd had a holiday or two at Skegness when I was much younger but, apart from that, my travelling had been severely limited. The idea of going to Liverpool appealed to me (I had checked an atlas and discovered it was close on a hundred miles from Nottingham) and I was pleased when there seemed a lot of others eager to go. On and off the proposed trip became a talking point from the dark days when the notice was posted until the Friday before the outing. On that Friday the talk was about little else.

I'd had a holiday or two at Skegness when young.

It meant I had to catch an earlier train than usual on the Saturday morning, and it was my first experience of relying on my father's built-in alarm clock. 'I shall wake you at half-past five,' he said to me the night before. 'That'll give you time to have a bit of breakfast and be at the station in good time to catch your train to Nottingham.'

My father, I later learned, had the amazing ability to sleep and wake at will and on the Saturday morning in question he came into my bedroom a minute or two before half-past five, shook me and told me it was time to get up. For once I needed no second calling. Mam insisted I had a good breakfast even though I was almost too excited to eat. At just turned six o'clock I was off, striding down the empty streets.

A week or so before – with the outing in mind – my mother had taken me along to the local Co-op and I was rigged out in a light grey sports coat, grey flannels (the bottoms of which were as wide as possible) and a blue-grey trilby. If one could be a masher at 15 then it was me. I reclined on the compartment seat of the early morning train and prayed there would be no breakdown or other incident that might delay my reaching Nottingham Midland station on time. The morning promised a fine day, I had my new clothes on, my ticket to Liverpool and back was in my pocket, the local train chugged on uneventfully, and a few minutes before seven o'clock drew into the station. I stepped on to the platform and felt this really was living.

'Be on platform five no later than 10 minutes past seven,' read the instruction on the notice and I quickly made my way there.

I was in good time but already most of the party had arrived. Gone were the overalls shiny with blacklead, the trademark of the twisthands and threader-lads. Instead there were suits of blue and brown, well cut most of them and bought to last. Good solid jobs, like the machines among which the wearers spent most of their time. There were one or two light greys or pale blues but they were very much in the minority, worn by the dashing young chaps who were unattached and had a pound or two in their pockets. 'I see you've got your 'at on, Mark,' one of the youngsters said. 'Well, it'd be no good 'im lending it to yo',' a mender quipped; 'yo'd nivver get it on your big 'ead.'

And so the great day started for the Peggoty gathering. Slowly the train pulled out of the station. We were in two long open-style coaches, four seats to a table. It was an ideal arrangement, giving us a sense of belonging, being part of a family. The early promise of a fine day looked like being fulfilled and some of the girls slipped off their coats and revealed an assortment of summer frocks. They were sporting their glad rags, pleased to be able to show they could wear something other than the long black overalls that were so much a part of the Peggoty scene.

The journey to Liverpool was memorable for me, chiefly because of Richard Budd and Lizzie Tatlow. Richard, a west of England man – he originated from Chard and had moved to Nottingham when there was a shortage of work in his part of the world – was a gentleman ever. At work his overalls were always cleaner than the rest of the twisthands'. He wore an overall *suit* of blue trousers and jacket, an outfit that set him a bit apart. He was the man given the job of making quality net used in the manufacture of wigs. He had the job because he could be relied on to turn out impeccable workmanship. If there was something wrong with his work (and it was inevitable that at some time or other even he would make a piece of net that contained a fault or two) it was a personal blow to his pride and he would appear at the office almost in tears as he explained to Jack Preston what he thought had gone wrong with his machine.

Richard sat on the train that Saturday morning, for a long time wearing his raincoat and bowler, almost as if he wanted to be neat and ready should any emergency arise and he had to get off in a hurry. But after a while he leaned across to me, his pink unlined face wearing a slightly embarrassed expression. 'Excuse me,' he said and he tottered off to the end of the long compartment. Andrew Paige, his twisthand son-in-law, jerked his long thin body half out of his seat and across to me. 'You'll 'ae to make allowances,' he said, 'it's 'is bladder.' And before we pulled into Liverpool Richard went off a few more times, his embarrassment becoming less as he worked himself into his necessary routine.

The old hands at these outings moved around a bit, dropping into a vacant seat here and there as the fancy took them. It was all new to me and I was glad to keep to my corner and remain as insignificant as possible. There were loud guffaws from the tables where pontoon was in progress, and the guffaws got louder as the bottles of beer – inevitable companions – began to take effect.

It was on one of Richard Budd's water journeys that Lizzie Tatlow came and dropped into his seat. I was to know Lizzie a good many years but she always seemed to me a slightly battered 25. She was not good-looking by any means, but she had a crude impishness that, over the years, enabled her to survive three husbands and more than her fair share of trouble. She was a pretty rough customer and when she had been talking to me half an hour (Richard, seeing his seat was occupied, found accommodation elsewhere) certain gaps in my education had been filled.

It was the fashion that summer for young women to wear hats not unlike the shallow-crowned bowler made famous by George Robey. But where the comedian's hat sat straight on his head, the lasses wore theirs diagonally and covering one ear. The 'in' colour was tan, although 'in' was a word not to be used in that connection for some years to come.

Lizzie was wearing her hat in the approved style and trying to look as if both it and her long tan coat were nothing very special, and to give the impression she was prepared to throw both hat and coat (and anything else) off without a second's hesitation should the mood take her. In my 15-year-old innocence Lizzie's highly-coloured stories had a blistering effect. I had heard a thing or two at the mineral water factory but Lizzie had all that beaten before the end of the first 10 minutes. Not that *she* seemed to be in any way aware that the world I'd known a short time before would never be the same again. Her parting shot I remember well. 'Men!' she said, in her most withering tone, 'I could write a book. I've bin wi' plenty, so I should know what I'm taking about.' And off she went to enliven one of the card schools. Richard Budd rejoined me after a while. He was quiet for a long time, old blue eyes staring out of the window, and then he said: 'A rum lass that one, a real rum lass.'

In Liverpool the pace seemed a good deal faster than anything back home. It wasn't, I suppose, but this was a great port and I wanted to be impressed. And the chosen restaurant was bigger than any I'd seen. Fortunately, my mother having been 'out service', as the term was, I'd been taught which piece of cutlery to use with the various dishes and felt a quite unjustified superiority when one of the threader-lads sitting nearby used his dessert spoon to drink his soup. But I didn't feel superior among the adults. One of them said: 'They've altered this place since I was here before.' I knew then there were other places than Nottingham and that some of the men sitting around me knew a thing or two about the world. This was living, I told myself again, and felt glad I was on the party.

Jack Preston, I was to learn afterwards, had asked old Charlie Searlby – who had a withered leg and walked with a pronounced limp – if he would keep an eye on me. Charlie had agreed, but he never made it obvious that he was to be my guide and mentor for the day. When we went through the Mersey tunnel he kept suitably silent and allowed me to take it all in, but when we crossed the river he pointed out first one building and then the other, dropping names as though they were old friends.

The bus tour in the afternoon allowed us to spend a bit of time wandering around the dockland area and moored there was the magnificent *Ark Royal*. One or two of the party carefully lined up their Box Brownie cameras, but no sooner had they done so than a man in uniform strode purposefully towards us waving his arms. 'No, no!' he shouted, 'no photographs!' Charlie, who always professed a knowledge of current affairs, said the would-be photographers should have known better than to try and snap something so secret and he hinted that we were only at the beginning of dark events. It was generally acknowledged at Peggoty's that he knew a bit more about the world than most folk. 'There might be one or two o' these lads serving on her before they're much older,' he said as we walked away.

Having viewed the *Ark Royal* from afar it was a treat when we were taken over the SS *Montclare*. 'This was the ship Crippen was caught on,' one of the

The works party, pictured aboard the SS *Montclare*, June 1938.

party said. 'Oh no,' said Charlie Searlby in measured tones. 'He was picked up aboard its sister ship, the *Montrose*.' To which came the reply: 'I wouldn't argue wi' yo', Charlie. An' I bet that cunning little bugger didn't argue either, when they grabbed 'im.' But it all impressed me. I bought a picture postcard of the ship and felt I had gleaned a priceless bit of information as we trooped off to tea.

George Bainbridge sat opposite me and kept his cap on throughout the meal. Surprisingly, nobody seemed to take any notice. My curiosity must have showed because Andrew Paige said to me as we trooped through to the gents afterwards: 'I've known George a few years and he's allus had his 'at on. He ain't got an 'air on his 'ead.' Another little mystery was solved.

In the evening, wandering around the city, Charlie once again had me in tow. He tried to make our walkabout interesting and was rewarded when we saw four Chinamen, complete with pigtails and small round hats. 'I see the coppers walk about in twos,' he said. 'So it's not only Broad Marsh that takes a bit of looking after.' The evening must have dragged a bit for Charlie. Not that he gave any hint of boredom, but later we bumped into some of the Peggoty party. 'Hello, Charlie, been for a drink?' 'No, haven't been able to,' Charlie said quietly – and I realised why. I felt guilty; growing up was taking a long time.

But there was plenty of boozing ahead for those who wanted it and Charlie would be able to slake his thirst when we set off for home. Whatever else might be missing from the outing it wouldn't be liquid refreshment. Even at the end of a long day's drinking, room could usually be found for a few more pints. I had to be content with lemonade but with Lizzie and a few others there was enough spice in their talk to intoxicate a Puritan.

The party became riotous as we sped through the night, but sleep claimed first one and then another until snores came from heads in all sorts of odd positions and the only ones awake stared glassily in front of them, drained of all effort at the end of a tiring day.

When we got to Nottingham in the early hours of Sunday morning I was able to add the finishing touch by bidding all and sundry a loud cheerio and stalking off to a waiting limousine. I tried to make it look as if I was used to being met by the family chauffeur.

Chapter Four

It's nice to dream when you're 15, but the truth was that my mother had arranged with our landlord for me to be met off the train. The landlord's son, then in his late 20s, was standing beside the car as our party straggled and stumbled up the steps at the station and out into the cool morning air. If he'd doffed his cap I couldn't have been more honoured. He was courtesy itself as he held open the door for me. No doubt he had summed up the situation and wanted to add his own bit of fun.

We sped off into silent Carrington Street and I waved like some pampered prince to the commoners with whom I had deigned to share the day. It was to be more than 20 years before I owned a car and then it was to be nothing more flashy than an old-type Ford Popular with springing that made you all too conscious you were riding. So perhaps it was simply a case of being king (nothing like a bit of swift promotion!) for a day. And the cost for me to be met and taken home in what was unheard-of luxury? Exactly one pound! And for that my chauffeur would have clocked nothing less than 35 miles and lost half a night's sleep. It must have been quite a sacrifice by my parents to raise that sort of money when there was so little coming into the family coffers.

Chapter Five

THE Liverpool trip was my first Peggoty outing but it was by no means my last and it became my responsibility after the war to do the organising.

A weekend in Majorca, a day in Paris (where you can be sitting high up in Montmartre at six in the evening and be tucked up snugly in bed by midnight, not a dozen miles from where Robin Hood roamed) is no more unusual today than a Saturday afternoon hike, but just before and after the war a day out could be quite an event. There were plenty among the Peggoty crowd who might never have seen the sea had it not been for works outings.

Things did improve a bit later on for the Mitchie sisters, but our trips were real red-letter days for them. Their working attire was black or something almost as sombre. The enormous hatpins they sported, with shiny end-stops, were the only bit of colour relieving their funereal outfits. Marvellous workers the pair of them – slaves, I suppose, by today's standards – and when they went on one of the firm's trips they were out to enjoy themselves. Not that they were ever likely to break into a jig or tell a risqué story, but they'd laugh or clap at somebody else's efforts. And they always managed to get themselves into situations that caused a few chuckles all round.

The first post-war outing was arranged for the middle of the week – and it was free into the bargain! We must have been doing pretty well that year. The privations most people had endured were beginning, bit by bit, to be shed. The gloom was lifting and there was a hint of prosperity around the corner. And the Wednesday we set off for Belle Vue, Manchester, was a day of sunshine and serenity. Even the normally exuberant threader-lads seemed content to sit and play their cards quietly.

But the train was rather full and, although we had a reserved vestibule carriage, with plenty of labels stuck on the windows announcing we were a private party, one man came aboard at Matlock, walked into our carriage with a rather supercilious air, and sat down in an empty seat at the Mitchie sisters' table. We were all comfortable enough and no one, least of all the sisters, seemed to mind the intrusion. So the man settled in and began to read his paper.

The Belle Vue outing where the Rhythm Sisters got lost.

As usual, there was plenty of beer on board and our Matlock friend hadn't been long among us when the Mitchies decided it was refreshment time. Mabel tottered along to the end of the coach to collect beer and glasses. Neither sister was very agile and the beer took a fair amount of jolting on the way from case to table. Jennie, not the brightest soul of the party – she spoke only when spoken to and then only in monosyllables – gallantly tried to do her bit and open a bottle. She battled with the stopper and managed to unscrew it just enough for the froth to come fizzing out in a long jet – which was aimed straight at the man who had been bold enough to sit opposite her. If he'd kept his paper up he might conceivably have weathered the sudden storm. But he didn't. He threw it down and jumped up, not knowing what had hit him. And as he fought to get out of his seat and started to hop about in the aisle down the centre of the coach, Jennie, as if hypnotised by his movements, turned after him, keeping the hissing liquid firmly trained on him until Mabel grabbed the bottle and screwed down the stopper.

'Damn you! Damn you!' the man cried, turning several shades of red and purple. Mabel, who was all apologies, picked up the now discarded morning paper and tried to wipe down the erstwhile immaculate suit of the stricken traveller. Jack Preston did his best to intervene but the man, now beside himself with rage, would have none of it and groped his dishevelled way out of the coach, cursing hard and smelling strongly of pale ale.

It wasn't really the Mitchies' day. They did their best to get lost in the Belle Vue grounds and when lunch was served they were reported missing. A search party found them going as fast as their corns and bunions would allow in the opposite direction to the arrow pointing to the dining hall.

But they were outing regulars and if they provided a laugh or two (they were called the Rhythm Sisters by the rest of us) they enjoyed themselves in the process.

Strange, though, how some of the Peggoty crowd couldn't bring themselves to go on the trips. 'Wait until we have this free do,' someone said, 'they'll all turn up.' But they didn't – and those who stayed at home tried to form a delegation to press the case for each dissenter to be paid a sum equivalent to the cost of the outing per person.

And there were the usual moaners, who said they would have been glad to go anywhere but the place selected. If the trip was to Cleethorpes they would have preferred Scarborough. If it was Bridlington they would have gone had it been Hunstanton. Somehow we could never get it quite right for them. Even when it was dear old Skegness there were usually one or two missing links. Skeggy was always a popular choice, although we had our problems.

There was the occasion when we had enough workers and their relatives to fill two buses. The first stop, as usual, was Newark market place, about

Chapter Five

A happy interlude on New Brighton sands.

15 miles into our journey. 'All off, the half-pint bladder merchants,' Jack Preston called, and away trooped half a dozen of the elderly men, among whom, inevitably, was Johnny Hopley. Johnny liked his beer, was always one of the first to start on his ration, and then was forever jigging up and down wondering if he could manage.

Before the coast was reached there had to be another stop; the main objective always seemed to be how much beer could be consumed in the time allotted.

One old publican had the surprise of his life when we pulled up at his tiny wayside inn. It was the sort of summer morning you dream about: sun shining out of a still blue sky and with that calmness about that can make England a green and pleasant land. The publican's wife was dusting the minute bar. 'Morning,' she smiled as the first few went indoors. And then, as more and more joined the leaders her eyes grew wider and wider. The little room was filled to overflowing and suddenly she turned and fled screaming: 'I'll tell 'im, I'll tell 'im!' She flew out through the back door and into the garden.

When she returned with her husband, a large and florid man, the pair of them stared unbelievingly. The old man took off his straw hat and stuffed the kidney beans he had gathered into the large pocket of his old smock. Our party had by this time filled the bar and spilled into the dining room; not that they had been invited into the private quarters; but they were there and there they were obviously going to stay.

'Well, I just hope I can serve you all, ' the old man said.

'Don't you worry about that, granddad,' Jack Preston told him, 'we'll serve ourselves.'

'Ar, but it's my reg'lars see. I must have enough for them,' the publican muttered as he tried to cope. He was used to service of a more leisurely kind, where he could pour a glass or two and then lapse into a bit of rustic conversation. Not so this morning. Thirsts were demanding attention and the old man simply wasn't fast enough. The company started to chant and the hint was taken. ''Ere, help yourselves and then tell me what I've sold. I'm going off to gather some more beans.' And he left us to it, with Jack Preston and me doing the necessary and the Peggoty brigade knocking back the old man's store.

Eventually we left. I reckon there had never been 60-odd in the pub before – certainly not at one time – and it's doubtful if there ever would be again. If the publican had been young it might have given him ideas and helped him to see there might be something in the tourist trade. But not that morning. As we climbed aboard he mopped his brow and, with his utterly bewildered wife, thankfully waved us on our way.

What was it, I wonder, that made works outings such glorified pub crawls? (It has to be in the past tense because, with so many car owners, such get-togethers are no longer the attractions they were.) Was it because they thought it the thing to do? Or was it the fact that lads and lasses (of whatever age) were out together and free for a few hours of their responsibilities? Certainly all the Peggoty outings were boozy 'do's'.

At Skegness the men invariably made for a pub that was home from home. The beer was brewed in Nottingham and more than once I heard somebody say: 'Well, there's one thing. We're sure of a good drink in t'Shades.' On one occasion I had arranged for luncheon to be served at 12.30 and at the appointed time there were only the women and one or two male teetotallers in sight. Most of the men were nowhere to be seen. 'Try the Shades,'

Destination Skegness, with a memorable pub call on the way.

somebody advised. I did and there they sat – the entire missing contingent – all gathered around the bar, like men who'd never seen a pint, or who had seen too many. I got them out, lunch was served, and another trip had been well and truly launched.

After lunch there was an hour or two when the drinkers would either sleep in deck chairs or find a bit of energy and try and recapture their lost youth with a jaunt around the fun fair. Fred Tinker, Jimmy Tatlow and Harold Hoxton, I remember, eyed the big dipper a bit warily but decided to have a go. I went with them. The least I expected was to see one of them pass out en route; but all went well until we reached the highest point before the long descent. Fred, all five feet five, 16 stone of him, sitting in the front seat, suddenly slipped back until he was lying almost flat. And that was the way he remained for the rest of the ride. He was so obese it wasn't possible for him, once down, to regain the normal sitting position. As he staggered off he adjusted his flat cap. 'I thought that bloody dentist had got me again,' he said. 'That were just how he had me in his chair'.

It was always a bit of a problem getting the company together for a photograph to be taken before starting out, assembling them for meals and

No lace factories at peaceful Skeggy.

making sure they understood the instructions regarding the time and place of return. There was one particularly anxious time, again at Skegness. It concerned Nellie. When she came to us from the Employment Exchange she handed in a card that stated she was a post-leucotomy patient. I had read that leucotomy was surgery where an incision was made into the frontal lobe of the brain to relieve some kinds of mental disorder. At the side of her head I noticed a mark, no doubt where a cut had been made. But she was fit for work it seemed, was taken on, and did the simple jobs given to her satisfactorily. When the summer outing was arranged Nellie's name appeared on the list.

It was arranged that the Rhythm Sisters should take care of her. They had managed quite adequately during the day but after tea she had given them the slip and was missing when it was time for the return journey. We waited for a while and made enquiries, but Nellie was nowhere to be found. We obviously couldn't hang around all night, so we decided to call in at the police station, report what had happened and, with some misgivings, go home.

The police took a full description of Nellie and our coaches pulled off into the night. It was early next morning that Jack Preston had a phone call from the police. They had found Nellie at a little village close on 10 miles from Skegness. She was walking home, she said. The police took her back to Skegness, bedded her down for the night and suggested to Jack Preston that he should send a taxi for her. He agreed, and the bill was presented to the firm for eight pounds. 'That would have bought me enough booze for a month,' Fred Tinker said. (In those days it would.) But it did, at least, save the wear and tear on Nellie's feet.

When the initial notice announcing that the following year's trip would be to Great Yarmouth was put up, enthusiasm was noticeably lacking, so we stuck a second notice up proclaiming FINE WEATHER GUARANTEED OR YOUR MONEY BACK! 'That'll cost you a few weeks' wages,' Jack Preston said to me with a grin. 'Aye, you too,' I replied. But from time to time we sold waste nylon and cotton to a merchant in the town who dealt strictly in cash and over a number of months we were able to build up a tidy float. 'We'll use that if we have to,' Jack said, 'but it'll mean we'll be short for the Christmas party. And I wouldn't want to miss that, especially if it was as good as last year's.' He laughed at the recollection.

Our Christmas parties always concluded with a raffle, with prizes of anything from a box of chocolates to a turkey. There was something for everybody and, last year, when Ruby Briddles crept in behind the others for the prize draw she made it on unsteady legs to a stool at the front from which, seconds later – port and lemon having its effect – she crashed to the floor, legs in the air. She might have been inebriated but her native wit didn't desert her and she said to the chairman of the group that had taken over the firm: 'I was hoping for a bottle, dearie, but now you've seen the colour of me pants I'll settle for a box of soapflakes.'

But back to Yarmouth... We started off, photograph taken, from Nottingham Midland station – and it was raining. 'Ah yes,' I told those who reminded me of the prophecy, 'don't worry: it's been fixed.' I had taken the trouble to ring the local weather station and was told there was a 50–50 chance it would be a fine day. That seemed a fair gamble, bearing in mind the English weather, but I just hoped there was enough in the cash float because Yarmouth had suddenly become a very popular place with the Peggoty crowd: there was a full turn-out.

After the weather the booze was the important thing and the old boys in

Off to Great Yarmouth, where the sun appeared to order!

the party had started drinking before we had gone more than a dozen miles. It couldn't have been much later than eight o'clock when somebody set the proceedings going with: 'Is t'bar open?' It wasn't, but a minute or two later it was. Beer, glasses, playing cards, fags – all the customary impedimenta of a works outing – appeared as if by magic. Peggoty's was on the move. And still it rained. The train chugged on and we ran into Norfolk under leaden skies. We pulled into the station. It was still raining but nothing like a few miles back. And then, unbelievably, as the last one or two old folks staggered on to the platform and the half-empty crates were organised for the return journey, the rain stopped. *It had actually stopped.* What is more, the sun showed signs of peeping through. Old Johnny Hopley looked up to the heavens: 'I shall have sommat to say to Thee one o' these days. If You'd kept it going for a bit longer we could have 'ad a free do today.' 'Ah, you've no faith, Johnny,' said Jack Preston. And then, to me: 'Bit of a miracle that, wasn't it?'

We dispersed, some to carry on their interrupted drinking, some to go the fun fair, some to the beach and others for a gentle stroll around the town – all to meet again for lunch. The meal was good, the sun shone, and there were smiles all round.

We played putting, had our ice creams and candyfloss, and then decided to go for a sail. All, that is, in our little party except May Carney. She fully expected to be seasick before we got out of the harbour (she had her Scarborough and Bridlington trips to prove her susceptibility) but at Yarmouth she beat all records. She merely looked at the boat tied up waiting to be boarded by trippers and riding the slight swell almost imperceptibly. May looked for a moment or two as if hypnotised and then disappeared. When she was next seen she looked a green two shades paler than the grass. We laid her on a seat in the shade while we went for a sail, with her head turned away from the sea.

And still the sun shone: through our sail, while we got together for tea, while we strolled about during the evening and as we started on the long ride home.

When one has started knocking beer back at just gone eight in the morning, and swilled it down at all possible opportunities during the day, it is more than surprising to find it can be looked at as the stars come out, blistered feet kick off shoes and tired heads begin to nod. But some of the hardened old twisthands were still able to bend their elbows with enthusiasm. It was their religion to drink while ever there was ale available.

We usually made an arrangement that everyone going on the outing was supplied with a specified number of tallies stamped with the name of the firm. Each one of these, according to colour, represented a bottle of either beer or mineral water. When their counters had gone the heavy drinkers started hunting around among those who were not so fond of the stuff to see if a deal could be done to the advantage of both parties. It was usually managed. In addition to the bottles for which tallies had been issued there were usually a few crates for sale.

On the journey home from Yarmouth both Jack Preston and I fell asleep. Or, to be really truthful, Jack fell asleep and I closed my eyes but was well aware of what was going on. 'They've both nodded off,' Fred Tinker said. Fred's capacity for ale – even by Peggoty standards – was bordering on the phenomenal. 'Come on,' he said, 'let's see 'em off.' Through half-closed eyes I watched them. We'd had a spanking day, the firm could afford the few bob involved, and it would round off the proceedings nicely to allow a bunch of hard-working cronies to think they'd had a few drinks for nothing. So I let them get on with it. The bottles were emptied and the 'dead men' returned to the crates.

When I knew the operation had been completed I went along and said: 'Anybody care for a drink? Come on, let's get rid of what's left.'

'I'll buy a couple,' Fred Tinker said and winked at his table companions. I played the game along with them, staring in mock disbelief at the crates, with not a full bottle to be seen. 'Come clean,' I said, 'who's downed all this beer?' 'We've been waiting for you to wake up and serve us,' said the irrepressible Fred. 'If there's nowt left it's because you've made a bloomer. You've miscounted. Any road, I've had enough for one day and it'll save me a couple o' bob.' 'Funny,' I said, 'I could have sworn we'd more than covered.' 'Aw, go and get your head down.' I did and when I returned to my seat there was uproar at Fred's table. We never mentioned the beer again, but Fred often asked afterwards if we were going to Yarmouth on our next trip. 'Best day out I ever had,' he said.

Chapter Five

Years after my first Peggoty trip to Liverpool we went again and on that occasion we included Birkenhead. Charlie Searlby was now an old man looking forward to his retirement and he preferred pottering in his greenhouse to sweating and struggling on an outing. But I thought of him as we crossed the Mersey and of the way he had aired his knowledge nearly 20 years before.

There was always some incident that put its mark on a Peggoty trip. It was Derby Day and on the train we ran a raffle. Everybody eagerly pitched in with their two bobs and that, for those days, made it a pool worth winning. Old Lizzie Glover – she'd been the office cleaner at the works for years, following Mrs Mallison – was one of the party and when I went round with their tickets she would insist on buying two. 'One's for me and one's for our Winkle,' she said. Winkle was her cat, a brute of quite enormous proportions, certainly the biggest cat I had ever seen.

We were walking along the front at Birkenhead just after three o'clock and we stopped a man who had a portable radio. 'What's won, mate?' 'Pinza,' he said, 'Gordon's managed it at last.'

Lizzie was on the edge of the crowd. Suddenly she shouted. 'Pinza? Did somebody say Pinza? That's our Winkle's horse!'

Lizzie had suffered from varicose veins for years but she forgot all about them in the excitement of the moment. She picked up her skirts and did a jig right there on Birkenhead front, singing as tunelessly as only she could: 'Our Winkle's won the Derby! Our Winkle's won the Derby!' Gordon Richards, I'm sure, would have been delighted!

If it were possible to reassemble the old Peggoty crowd and ask them which place was first in their affections, it would be a close call between Skegness and Blackpool, with Blackpool perhaps just edging in front. 'We shall have to organise a day at Blacky,' Jack Preston would say. 'Let's go and see the lights.'

Off we would go on an October Saturday morning and get within touching distance of the Tower before midday. Lunch would follow at some pre-arranged spot, then football in the afternoon if Blackpool were at home, and then a long steady stroll along the length of the illuminations soon after tea. There would be anything up to a dozen of us arm-in-arm, with even the

Off to Blackpool, to see the lights and watch Stan Matthews.

weakest quips starting off peals of laughter. It was hilarity for the sake of it. 'We laughed at nowt,' as one of the party once said. For when we were away on an outing we imbibed something of the spirit of the many Lancastrians who treat Blackpool as their Mecca. Work was left behind for a bit and if you couldn't relax in Blackpool it was a poor tale.

I shall always treasure the memory of the first time I saw Stanley Matthews play. That Saturday afternoon he lived up to everything I had read or heard about him. His game began quietly enough, with him trying to go on the outside of the marking defender. Then he started to go on the inside and time after time he beat the full-back, so much so that the Sheffield man (it was Blackpool playing Sheffield Wednesday) became increasingly frustrated and was finally reduced to holding the great Stan by his shirt in an effort to halt the magic. It was the jinking, elusive Matthews of legend.

On that day all for once had gone perfectly with the Peggoty party – until the redoubtable Ruby Briddles missed her footing getting out of the carriage as we pulled into home. One minute she was there, with her Kiss Me Sailor hat perched on her head. Then she lay sprawled on the platform, her ankle twisted and unable to bear her weight. There seemed to be only one practical solution. We loaded her on to a porter's trolley, wheeled her along the platform and on to the goods lift. She lived close to the station and, with the blessing of British Railways, we trundled her home. Her pain had subsided a bit and she suddenly went into hysterical laughter as she lay flat out under the stars.

'My old man'll never believe it,' she wailed. 'He'll think the railway's delivering a bloody parcel!'

Chapter Six

ON THE top floor of the factory, in a long narrow room, with windows the whole length and on either side, were the slip-winding frames. It was here that Italian and Japanese silk, cotton from Egypt, artificial silk and – later – nylon were run from the hank, cheese or spool on to wooden bobbins of the right size to fit the spindles on the brass-bobbin winding creels. All of which sounds highly technical, but it isn't. Most trades have their own peculiar terms and ours was no exception. The hanks were simply long, long lengths of continuous thread, and cheeses, spools and cones were different sizes and packages of – again – continuous thread of varying yarns. Slip-winding frames were simple belt-driven contraptions for winding from the packages on to wooden bobbins; and the brass-bobbin engines were machines worked by highly-skilled operators who filled two paper-thin discs of brass (that were riveted together) with the yarn that had been so carefully wound by the slip-winders.

If slip-winding was a monotonous operation (although the operatives never seemed to complain) there was the compensation of doing it in this long, light room with a view. It became very hot in summer, very cold, save when the heating system was working well, in winter; but from half-past seven in the morning until half-past five in the evening the handful of winders did their work. They were standing most of the time and their days must have been long and tiring.

For years – certainly before the war – it seemed a section of the factory apart from the rest and there always appeared to be an air of subservience. It was a throwback from the even more severe days that had gone before. On a summer morning, with the sun shining strongly over the River Trent and the whole room bright with golden light, it would have been hard to imagine a better place in which to work. A better place in a factory, that is. And the occupants of the room, if you observed them closely enough, certainly seemed a bit more spry on such days.

But the summer sun did nothing to dispel the atmosphere of servitude, made worse by the dark and sombre clothes the women wore. Mabel and Jennie Mitchie, for instance: grey frocks as a change from black but always black stockings and shoes. They might give way now and then to coloured pinafores – bright by their standards but that would do little to relieve the general picture. Jennie always wore a black beret as well, although it had been

Mid-morning break at the factory.

known for Mabel to sport a hat adorned with a flower, and there was the inevitable thumping great hatpin protruding either side of her head, as if to proclaim to the world that once her hat was on it was there to stay.

I don't know how long the Mitchies had been at Peggoty's, but they must have done near enough 80 years' service between them. When I first knew them in the summer of 1936 Mabel was drawing the princely weekly wage of one guinea; sister Jennie – certainly not as bright as Mabel – was paid 17 shillings and sixpence. Mabel was assistant overlooker and knew the job inside out.

Eliza Dunmore was in charge of the slip-winders. She was a tall and regal spinster who, I thought later, would have looked well in the part of Miss Moffatt, the schoolmistress in Emlyn Williams' play *The Corn is Green*. But it is doubtful if Eliza had ever been inside a theatre, let alone on the stage. She always wore a long black dress and was as Victorian in outlook as Victoria herself.

She must have been all of five feet ten tall and her back was ramrod-straight. She was the overlooker and let's have no nonsense about it. There were only six or seven slip-winders in the room but when it came to break time Eliza sat apart from them. Mixing with the rank and file never became even a remote possibility. There never for the slip-winders – architecturally nearer to heaven then any of the others in the factory, with the exception of Charlie Barnwell – any chance of laughter or levity while Eliza was hovering near. It must have been quite a relief when she went downstairs to the office on one of her rare visits. She invariably treated Jack Preston with a deference she thought his due and it was unthinkable that she would ever do less than a full day's hard work, or allow others to. She had a rigid code of conduct and, as far as she was concerned, there was a proper pecking order. If Jack Preston had to be obeyed by her, so those in her room must be prepared to do her bidding.

I wondered sometimes what sort of life she lived outside her working hours. She lived with Miss Willars, overlooker before her, and who, according to those who had worked under her, had been a martinet. When Miss Willars died Eliza lived on in the house alone. How alone I never knew because there seemed to be an impenetrable barrier around her. Never once did I hear of any friends and whenever there was a day's outing for the Peggoty crowd she could never be tempted to go. Occasionally, during the war, I would get a letter from Jack Preston. One, when I was in Belgium, brought the news that Eliza had died and for a long sad moment that seemed more important than the V1s and V2s that were making life difficult.

In the same letter there was the statement that Mabel Mitchie was to become overlooker. I remember feeling pleased about that, but a bit apprehensive for Mabel. But her experience saw her through and when I returned to the factory, there she was bidding me welcome with her distorted grin. Jack Preston had plenty to criticise her for, so he said, but for the pittance she was paid the firm could not complain. She was probably in her mid-forties when I first knew her and had very little to thank the gods for. She had the appearance of having had a stroke: one side of her face was completely mis-shapen, her mouth sagged at one corner and one eye always showed red on the rim. She had difficulty in talking clearly and when she did speak her distorted cheek blew in and out. She had bad legs and in her later years walking must have caused her a great deal of discomfort. She was in the old mould of workers, afraid for their jobs, and if she happened to be sitting when anyone with the slightest authority went into her room she would jump up at once. Above anything, she must never be seen to be having even the briefest rest. Slip-winders were there to work; Mabel saw, like Eliza, that they did and she drove herself harder than any of them.

I was told that Mabel's appearance was caused, not by a stroke, but through having a tooth out. Whether that was true or not I never found out. I admired her for the way she made the best of things. She and her sister never had a real week's holiday but as soon as they knew the trip list was up their names were among the first to be appended.

When one of the brighter sparks in the factory dubbed them the Rhythm Sisters it was not unkindly meant. Jennie might not have had a clue what was intended but Mabel would and she would have laughed heartily enough. But it seemed fate was really dishing the bad blows out when one of the few bombs to be dropped on Nottingham landed near their home and injured Jennie. The firm paid her while she was in hospital – it surely couldn't have done otherwise – but Mabel's gratitude was quite touching and if she'd been told to kneel and kiss Jack Preston's feet it isn't difficult to imagine her doing so.

Touching, too, were the occasions when there would be a timid knock on the office door and Mabel would poke her head round. 'I'm sorry to bother you, Mark, but would you be good enough to fill in this 'ere tax form?' She had asked so many times that this was one question she was able to reel off pat. And because she knew the drill she would at the same time produce her insurance policies, ancient documents held together by enormous safety pins. It was a matter of a few minutes' work for me, but she always insisted on paying a couple of bob 'For your kindness and your trouble.' To have refused to take her payment would have been to insult her.

Firms like Peggoty's had been built on the labours of those such as Mabel but even stalwarts like her who seemed to alter so little over the years could not keep Old Father Time at bay for ever.

Attempts were made shortly after the war to modernise some of the methods of the firm and one of the first moves was to get understudies to certain people. Mabel was to train a bright and brash 20-year-old.

It was impossible for someone who had worked most of her life in a time of cheap industrial labour to view such a move without fear. There was no doubt in Mabel's mind that the girl was learning the job to replace her at the earliest opportunity. Mabel, to whom life had dealt a pretty tatty hand, was a fairly stoical character, but this proved too much. The distrust she had of authority was never far beneath the surface. Her destination, she was convinced, was the scrap heap. When she came to the office and cried she looked a pitiful figure. Jack Preston patiently explained the situation to her. 'Never,' he said, 'was it the intention to do anything to upset you. Your job, trade conditions permitting, is secure.' J.P. had once worked in the factory and he was trusted. Mabel dried her tears, her twisted smile reappeared and she climbed her painful way back to the top of the works.

(A thought here relevant to the previous paragraph. It is in no way surprising that the Labour movement and the Trade Unions have become so strong. Working conditions, particularly just before and after World War Two, were in many cases shocking. The Haves completely dominated the Have-nots. The two sections simply lived in different worlds. Maybe the pendulum has swung too far the other way now but it was always on the cards it would. At one time the Mabels of this world were ground

NOTTINGHAM

QUINCENTENARY
CELEBRATIONS

....

TRADE EXHIBITION

BROAD MARSH
JUNE 27th — JULY 2nd
1949

Lace Stands Nos. F6 & F7

Nottingham Laces

LEVERS MACHINE —

reproduces almost every type of hand made lace, as well as many beautiful hybrid types in wide ranges of quality and width, from narrow edgings to Allover nets and Flounces up to 54 inches wide : from cobwebby Chantillys to coarse, heavy napery laces, known as Torchons : from Veilings or Hair nets, to narrow Picots or Veinings.

For adornment of almost every feminine garment in every kind of yarn.

PLAIN NET MACHINE —

in different gauges produces nets in a wide variety of yarns and in various qualities. Coarse or fine mesh net can be made on one machine within the limits of the particular gauge. The machine will also make Point d'Esprit or Spotted net, used for blouses, dresses, etc. Silk, Rayon and Cotton tulles, Mosquito nets, nets for embroidery, for the brassiere, millinery and confectionary trades, and for theatrica lpurposes, to mention only a few of the uses to which these nets are put.

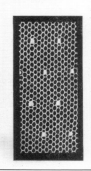

Laces displayed at the Nottingham Quincentenary Celebrations, Broad Marsh, 1949.

Nottingham Laces

SCHIFFLI MACHINE —

a second process machine in that it embroiders a net or material base. This base can either be permanent or subsequently dissolved in processing, giving a very wide choice of styles of reproduction, mainly of Needlerun and Guipure (burn-out) types.

Shapes and Motifs for lingerie adornment can be made in great variety on all kinds of basic materials and in every colour.

Allover designs are used for blouses, dresses, corsets and brassieres, etc.

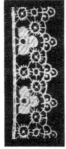

BARMEN MACHINE —

is a producer on a much smaller scale than either Levers or Schiffli machines, usually making only one breadth of lace at a time and that confined to the narrower widths. The style produced, although the nearest approach to hand made lace, is limited : mainly Torchons are made and used for underwear and napery, although it is capable of reproducing very closely hand made Valenciennes.

The Barmen machine has also successfully produced laces from elastic threads ; these are used for underwear and corsets.

WARP MACHINE —

a needle machine with a knitting or crocheting action. The laces it produces are chiefly of the crochet style. Nets, of varying meshes, are also made for special purposes, including :—Curtains, Millinery veiling in limited styles, Hair nets and corseting fabrics. Hat and shoe fabrics are also produced on this machine.

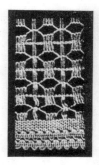

CURTAIN MACHINE —

apart from the Curtains and Curtain nets to be seen on Stand No. C 1, this machine produces fine Filet laces and Napery.

continuously into the dust and it is, I am sure, the memory of this – or accounts of it handed down – that plays a vital part in our thinking. What would the Mitchies have done if they had been given the sack (it wouldn't have been hard to find justification: shortage of work was a good standby) and joined the unemployed? They would have lived on a pittance – forever.)

It was common enough at Peggoty's to have more than one member of the same family working there. Dad spoke for his lad, brother for sister, uncle for nephew. Just as we had the Mitchie sisters, so we had the Leggatts, Edna and Phyllis. They came from a large family; Edna was a slip-winder and Phyllis a mender.

Edna had worked for Peggoty's since leaving school. I always felt sorry for her; she looked frail and downtrodden, in contrast to her big and bouncy younger sister. It was Edna who, determined to escape the terrible conditions in which the Leggatt family lived in the overcrowded St Ann's district, decided to let her boyfriend make love to her in the hope of becoming pregnant. Her plan worked. Freddy, the boyfriend, married her. Edna was able to move away, get a home of her own, raise a family and still keep working – apart from having time off to give birth. She was one of the Peggoty stalwarts. If she did slip from grace now and then in the matter of attendance it was because she had been out on the beer the night before and had simply overslept.

Hard-working though Edna was, she seemed incapable of budgeting her cash beyond the immediate future. Her horizon was bounded by the factory, home and pub. For all her frailty she drank enough over the years to sink the proverbial battleship, while Freddy accounted for the rest of the fleet.

Along with beer went the darts; darts then had not earned such widespread popularity. Edna, from all accounts, was a dab hand. Maybe that was because she was able to practise on the doorstep. She lived for years in a two-up and two-down terrace house near enough to her local to almost reach out from her front door and draw herself a pint.

The day when Phyllis said to me with great solemnity that Edna had a serious liver complaint and had only a few years to live seems like only the week before last, but it must be all of 40 years ago. I remember saying how sorry I was to get the news. And I was sorry, for she was a pleasant woman and, apart from the times when suffering the occasional hangover, a first-class worker. I thought of her young family and wondered how they would manage. And who would look after Freddy? He might appear a tough character but he had always clung to Edna. She, in spite of her pallid appearance, was the real backbone of the family.

But the years came and went and as each January the first came round so did Edna. Maybe the message I had received about her had been somewhat garbled. Had the medicos got it wrong, I wondered? In any event the subsequent 20 years saw Edna pickling the suspect organ in a fair amount of alcohol. Could it be that, failing to kill it, it had done the opposite and cured it?

Freddy, not to be outdone, spent a fair proportion of his time at the doctor's. He had a serious heart complaint, I heard, and had been given strict instructions to get off the booze. It was another case, obviously, of either not hearing the doctors correctly or proving their diagnosis wrong. For Freddy saw a pint pot as regularly as the moonlight he staggered home by, although it might disappear now and then in a cloud of cigarette smoke. For he smoked as much as possible in between his coughs.

The part of the city where Edna and Freddy spent so much of their married life has now been transformed. No longer do narrow streets house the bustling life that was such a colourful part of the scene not all that many years ago. Edna and Freddy have moved on, no doubt to somewhere conveniently close to a pub.

Is it simply an old wives' tale that what is bred in the bone comes out in the flesh? Or are some of the sociologists right when they say a change of environment can transform character? I wonder. Freddy and Edna had a bit of trouble with some of their children; one of them was more than a handful. Maybe she's steadied a bit over the years but at an early age she developed into an accomplished liar with a liberal daubing of childish charm to help her get into and out of enough scrapes to last a lifetime. Truancy from school was her abiding passion, but she would go home after a day spent mooching round the shops (with a bit of shoplifting thrown in) or going to the cinema (on money she had nicked from her mother's purse) and tell thoroughly convincing tales to her parents about the way she had spent her day at school. A pleasanter, more polite lass it would have been difficult to find.

At about the time Edna was planning to trap Freddy into marrying her, one of her workmates had herself been trapped. I was just a lad at the time and knew nothing until all the excitement was over. Anita was a good-looking woman of maybe 23 or 24, and was terribly shy. If you passed her on the stairs she hurried by close to the wall, never even glancing up. Oddly enough for one living in a city and working all day in a factory, she had a ruddy complexion and looked for all the world like a farmer's daughter.

One day she was missing. That was unusual because she was one of those who seemed never to be away. The following day she was back at work. It was not until much later that I heard she had stayed at home to have a baby. I never knew the truth of it really and I wouldn't have dared to make enquiries, but later conversations pointed to it being fact. They were hard times and folk didn't like losing a day's pay. But confinement and back to work 24 hours later was something I thought happened only to the Chinese – and Peggoty's was a long way from the nearest paddy-field.

Maybe it was the height at which they worked – probably seeing the clouds so much nearer than most other people – that had an effect on some of the slip-winders. Over the years the room had its share of characters.

The pleasant Yorkshire lass was one. She was with us for only a brief interlude, was as Yorkshire as Ilkley Moor and just about as rugged. She sang as she worked and had a voice as pleasing as her personality, but when she went off at the end of the day she would spend a full minute peeping up and down the street, keeping herself concealed in the employees' entrance until she was satisfied that all was clear. And then off she would run and her running had the same sort of vigour as her singing. Then, one day, we had a note from her. 'Please send my cards,' it read. 'He's found me. I shan't be coming back.'

Just as Ellen, a shy little woman who must have had her fair share of troubles, never came back. She walked out one lunchtime and we never saw her again. 'Was there some trouble with Ellen this morning?' I asked Mabel. I felt concern, for Ellen was as tragic a figure as the Yorkshire girl was comic. Mabel's lop-sided face wore an added look of sadness. 'Well, if you ask me she's been in a lot of pain lately. In fact, at one time this morning she was running up and down the room it were that bad.'

Chapter Six

'Why didn't you come to the office and phone for a doctor?'

'We wanted to but she wouldn't hear of it.'

Two or three days later we heard Ellen had died and shortly after that her husband appeared on the scene. He made a good effort at acting the part of the grieving spouse but it transpired he had left Ellen some years before and she, alone and broken, had been forced out to work. For a few years she had been cheerful enough. She was a clean, alert, hard-working little woman, but always on the defensive and carrying with her a permanent air of desolation.

Chapter Seven

TWISTHANDS are the men who work lace machines and in the early glory days, it is said, they were the trade's skilled workers – and knew it. 'Ah,' old Richard Budd would say, 'there were days I'm told when the twisthands would ride to work in carriages and pay their fare with golden sovereigns.' And his old blue eyes would take on a wistful look. Then he would say: 'I can tell you though, boy, it never happened in my day.' But the twisthands were usually men who had spent long years at their craft and knew how to handle their often temperamental machines.

When I went to Peggoty's in the 1930s most of the twisthands worked what were known as double-handed jobs. Just how they apportioned their hours was usually dependent upon how many machines they had and how well they worked with their butties. Two of the men at Peggoty's had seven or eight machines (slightly narrower machines than the norm) and they worked together through the day, starting at about half-past six in the morning and knocking off at about half-past six or seven at night. It was often said they couldn't stand the sight of each other, but with so many machines to look after there wasn't much time for falling out, and the only time they seemed to pause for a breather was for an hour each Friday morning when they cleaned their machines and shared the one wage packet for the job.

But there were some men who had only two machines between them. They worked single-handed and on split shifts, starting at five o'clock in the morning summer and winter and, hopefully, keeping their machines going until eleven o'clock before walking home under the stars. Two such butties were Andrew Paige and Johnny Hopley. For years, day in and day out they kept up their routine, each having implicit faith in the other. One man would come on at five, work until nine, go home for his breakfast, return to work at one o'clock. He would then work until six in the evening. The other man would start at nine, work until one, go home for lunch, and then reappear at six to work through until 11.

Why each man favoured working that way instead of carrying on for a straight nine hours I don't know. I did hear it said that the way they worked meant that if there was a bit of trouble on a machine the man due to go off home could stay and help his butty and wouldn't feel too jaded having had a break. Certainly the two men worked marvellously together. True enough, one would say of the other every now and then: 'He's left me a bloody fine mess to get cleared up,' or some such friendly comment, but I never knew them quarrel and their workmanship had to be good because they were strictly on their own time. If a machine stood, so did their money.

When I first went to Peggoty's artificial silk had just come to prominence. Cotton, which was the yarn used for many years, now slipped into second place. Nylon and other man-made fibres were still way in the future and the twisthands saw artificial silk as heralding a new day in their trade. As one old boy said to me: 'This is kid's play after working cotton. These old machines can go a bit now.' What he meant was that the machines went for longer without causing trouble. That, in turn, meant more money in the pay packets on Saturday morning, simply because there were more yards (or racks, as the standard measurement was called in the trade) to record.

One of the hazards of working cotton was the number of 'thicks' a twisthand had to put up with. A 'thick' was precisely what it said – a small length in the cotton yarn that was thicker than it should have been and stood every chance of lifting one of the wafer-thin brass bobbins and its surrounding holder (called a carriage) out of the path it was traversing, thus causing a machine smash. When that happened it meant the machine had to stand until the necessary repair had been carried out. That kind of thing didn't happen so much with artificial silk and for a pair of butties to have machines rattling away non-stop – as Andrew and Johnny often did – transformed their

One of the Raschel machines that took over a large share of modern lace production.

While the sun still shone: drawing, examining and jennying Nottingham lace, the product on which much of the city's fame was built, is shown in the next five pictures.

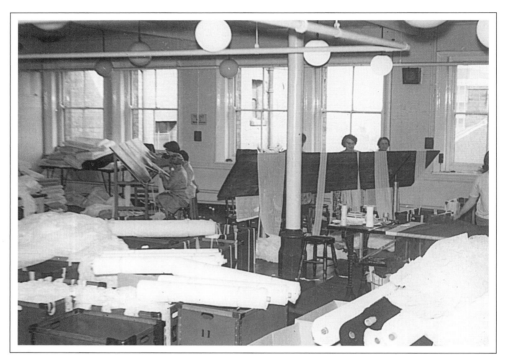

working life completely. They still had to know what made the job tick but their days were slightly less arduous.

Andrew and Johnny were keen, conscientious men. They had a tremendous loyalty to the firm and would be prepared to crawl to work even if they were below par. Financial considerations must have been a strong motivating force, but a fierce loyalty was there all the same. Even when they called each other – and inevitably they did – it did nothing to diminish the deep respect they had for the other's ability. And to make sure that ability was kept up to scratch and the work was up to an acceptable standard, there was Bess Skeet. If she saw a bad piece she would be on to the offenders like a ton of bricks. Too many faults could mean a man's wages being docked to help pay for the excess mending.

In Andrew's case there were a lot of mouths to feed. It would more often be mutton broth than pheasant pie, but the large family never went hungry. And Maisie, Andrew's wife, was always prepared to do an extra bit of mending at home should there be any chance of the old man not having much in his packet at the weekend.

Andy (it was only Jack Preston and me who called him Andrew) was more than six feet tall and thin as a pipe cleaner. He always rolled his shirtsleeves as high as possible and he had the thinnest arms I've ever seen. When he and Johnny were carrying warps (yarn – hundreds of yards of it – wound on to steel beams maybe four metres in length) down the necessary five flights of stairs, you felt that Andy would never manage it, and that his thin body would break under the strain.

Looking back it is a wonder the twisthands didn't revolt over the warp-carrying business. The warping shop was on the second floor, which meant at least 30 stone stairs had to be negotiated. The warp beams were almost vertical at times as the men worked their way round the staircase angles and then – in Andy and Johnny's case – there were about 60 yards on the flat through the factory yard before they reached their machines. But it was all part and parcel of the job and, of all the twisthands employed at Peggoty's, the attendance record of these two was second to none.

Andy's skinniness was made worse by the fact that he was terribly pale, had a hook nose and a bald head apart from a mass of hair low down at the back, giving the impression he was wearing a peculiar sort of ruff. He would peer at you over steel-rimmed glasses, move close when conversing, often looking over your shoulder when you were facing him – as though he wanted to be well aware of anyone approaching who might be interested in hearing his remarks. On the odd occasion when he walked hatless down the factory yard, striding out with his head well forward, he looked for all the world like a shortsighted bird of prey.

But it was a very rare occasion when he was seen without his hat. And a hat to Andy meant nothing else but a bowler. He had two bowlers: one, green with age and wear, he used for work; the other, his best, hung on the picture rail in the front room of his little terrace house.

It was always the proud boast of his wife that the money she earned from lace mending took the two of them on their annual holiday to Blackpool. They went for a week, year in and year out. A number of things were important to Andy. At one time he was a fervent Nottingham Forest supporter and one of the great delights of his life was a Saturday afternoon at the match, seeing Forest win and then going home to a huge plateful of mussels. 'The way to do 'em,' he told me more than once, peering with screwed-up eyes over my shoulder, 'is to feed 'em a bit of oatmeal and let 'em stand for a bit. Brings 'em on a treat, does oatmeal.' And then, after his tea, he would have a quiet drink with Maisie at a pub just around the corner from home, where his best bowler and her best hat were Saturday night landmarks.

I don't know how many times Andy and Maisie went on holiday to Blackpool but it must have run into dozens. They always reckoned it was their Blackpool week that set them up for the winter. 'Last year,' I remember Maisie telling me – and it wasn't long before she died – 'we were walking along t'front. Suddenly our old man turned to me and said: "What's everybody staring at?" "Staring at," I said to him. "They're allus likely to stare. It's you, you soft bugger, in that bowler. Fancy coming here in that."'

Rumour had it that Andy had said to Mr Skelhorn, when he knew he might be called up during World War One: 'I'd rather break my leg than go.' But he had to go and his pipe-stem frame survived intact. It was always said around the place that Andy had a bit of the bully in him. If he saw he could browbeat anybody he would. But if a man stood up to him there was never much danger. It was said his old woman was the one who put fire in his belly. And knowing them both I should say that was quite likely. But whatever one might say about Andy it could never be laid at his door that he was a man who shirked work. Whenever there was a pound to be got out of his machines he was there to get it. Much as he liked watching Nottingham Forest, going to Blackpool, wearing his bowlers, eating mussels, smoking a pipe, belching (at which he was particularly good) and moaning, his work was first-rate and he had no peers at Peggoty's when it came to effort. When one of his family was working for the firm and proving a pretty shiftless character, Jack Preston said to him with some heat: 'You're not fit to lick your old man's boots!'

But in Johnny Hopley Andy had a butty as good as himself. At the end of his working days he was able to say – because there came a day when he staggered down the factory yard, never to return – 'I've nivver had a day off work through illness.' In his day and age, when it really was the survival of the fittest, that was something of which he could be justly proud. I saw him more than once when he should have been home and in bed but working was his life and I think he must have had some odd idea that if he stayed away the magic would be broken. And so he kept going, walking to work and home again – the four journeys would notch up four or five miles a day – in all weathers, battered old felt hat on his head, shoulders hunched as he got older, coat collar turned up and very often, depending on the temperature, a dewdrop on the end of his nose. When he was well into his seventies he was still spry enough to run down the factory yard to the gents, a place high on his list of priorities as he got old. 'Drink one pint and pee three,' he would mutter.

At near enough 70 he could dribble a tennis ball in the yard with considerable artistry and many's the summer evening, when the threader-lads were waiting for work, that he would leave his machines for five precious minutes and take them on. Johnny, it was said, had once had a trial for Aston Villa and there seemed to be little doubt, as he nimble-footed it round three or four teenagers, that some soccer manager should have snapped him up. 'He were a bloody marvel at it,' Andy once told me, 'but t'game didn't pay owt like it does today, you know. And owd Johnny had a pretty good job and so he stuck it.'

Away from work Johnny and his wife were inseparable. They were devoted to each other, although to hear Johnny talk about her sometimes you wouldn't have got that impression. She had obviously been a good-looker in her day and still dressed smartly when I knew her. But as the years wore on she had spells when she was a bit off the beam and now and then she would turn up at the factory and tell Jack Preston, if the factory happened to be going through a lean spell, that he should bring down the price of his goods so that more could be sold. J.P. would tell Johnny that his wife had been to see him. Johnny would smile and shake his head, a look of utter resignation on his lined face. 'Oh dear,' he would say, 'our bloody old woman. I'm sorry. I'll talk to her when I get home.' And no doubt he would but it wouldn't make a scrap of difference. Whenever she thought her advice was needed she would appear again.

Johnny always drank cocoa at work and week in week out his old cracked jug would stand on the hotplate surrounding the furnace where Charlie Searlby kept the metal for casting parts of machine insides. When Johnny wanted to make a fresh lot of cocoa he would simply swill hot water round the jug, throw the resulting brown liquid away, and then make his new day's ration. The jug never had a proper wash but that didn't seem to bother him. He would wipe his mouth with the back of his hand when he had taken a few long swigs. 'Next to Shippo's bitter that's t'best drink you can get,' he would say.

He had false teeth and there were bits chipped off here and there. When he had his sandwiches at work – and they were mostly bread and butter (he insisted on butter) and huge pieces of Gorgonzola cheese – out would come his teeth. They would be placed on some convenient part of a machine while he walked up and down his alley, carefully watching the lace he was making and munching away while he kept surveillance. It was vital he should keep his machines going while he had his midday feed. Yardage on the clock meant everything.

On one occasion I went into his alley and there were his teeth, hideously stained, sitting on one of his machines. As I approached he picked up another sandwich, looked at it a bit dolefully and then turned to his teeth, holding the sandwich out to them. 'Here,' he said, 'can yo' lot manage this? I've had enough.'

Chapter Seven

Whenever they went on an outing Johnny and his wife would find a pub near the bus or railway station and, sitting side by side like a couple of turtle doves, with scarcely a word passing between them, sup their evening away. Johnny would puff contentedly at his pipe, only leaving his place to relieve himself (which was often) while his wife, in between sips of her stout, would sit staring into space, only muttering when Johnny spoke to her. She never seemed to leave her place at all. It was almost as if she was mechanical – sipping, staring, muttering, sipping, staring, muttering, until the time came for them to leave to catch either the bus or train home.

Such was the situation when we had a day in Manchester. A few of us were in the same pub as Johnny and his wife. It was quite near the railway station and had, in fact, been chosen by them for that reason. When we left we told them to keep a check on the time. Johnny acknowledged our warning with a flick of his pipe-stem – and that was the last we saw of them that night. We searched the railway station frantically but they were nowhere to be seen. We set off for home without them.

Next morning I went round to their little terrace house. Johnny grinned sheepishly when he came to the door. It was a relief to see him but I was curious to know what had happened. His wife appeared behind him in the tiny kitchen. 'It were him,' she said accusingly. 'His watch had stopped.' And that, it seems, was the story. Our train left at 9.45pm. Johnny was well aware of that and decided that if he and his wife left the pub at nine-fifteen they would have ample time. And so they would have. When he looked at his watch and saw it was only half-past eight he settled down with another pint of ale for himself and a glass of stout 'for the old woman.' They slowly downed their drinks: Johnny looked at his watch again and saw it was still half-past eight. But in truth it was nearer half-past nine. The extra pint caused him to make another trip outside. That had to be done whether he was late or not. And after that they were doomed. So we made a steady journey home without them. They followed a couple of hours later on a train that made innumerable stops and got them into Nottingham when dawn was breaking.

But Johnny's watch was going all right on Monday morning. It had to be. He was never late for work no matter what shift he was on.

Although Johnny never had a day off work through illness there did come a day – he was well past 70 at the time – when he was found in the alley between his machines staggering about and obviously far from well. 'You'd better go home,' we said gently. 'Put your things on and we'll get you a taxi.' He refused point blank. 'I shall be alright on t'bus.' His independence burned brightly. 'Besides, our old woman'll be all cut up if she sees me roll up in a taxi.' She had caused him a few anxious moments in her time but he would go to any lengths to avoid upsetting her. So we let him go, with one of the young lads set to trail him to see he made it home safely. The report came back that he had managed without mishap. We waited for his return but the magic thread had been broken. The old man never came back.

Priceless Lace Market buildings – soon to become attractively residential.

Chapter Seven

We learned afterwards that some weeks before Johnny had been to see his doctor, for the first time in many years. He must have been one of his GP's best customers. His visits could have been written on the back of a postage stamp. But within a few short months of the day he tottered down the factory yard for the last time he was dead.

These two, Andrew Paige and Johnny Hopley, were cast in the mould of the men who had made lace-making a craft industry. They had lived through good times and bad, although their good times would not have been reckoned so hot by today's standards.

Jobs before 1939 were hard to come by and most of the twisthands I knew had lived through spells of varying length when there was a shortage of work and they had to exist on the dole. What knowledge they had of the trade they hugged close to themselves. There were not many twisthands who would readily part with their secrets. True, the real skill was not simply what a man knew but how he employed what he knew. Many a good and conscientious man died with his secrets untold: the details of how to calculate how much a specific amount of yarn on his warp would make if the lace was to be a certain quality; what machine was best served by what material; how to weight complicated designs so that the resultant pattern looked good. Their secrets were often entered into little notebooks and jealously guarded, as like as not going with the twisthand when he left the factory for the last time. In the bad old days there were many more men than jobs and the protection of hard-won skill was the final fortification behind which a threatened craftsman could build his defence.

Chapter Eight

I N A way the canal (or 'cut' as it was usually called by the Peggoty workers) was as much a part of our life as the factory itself. It simply wouldn't have been the same place without that sluggish and uninviting stretch of water. As the years went by traffic on the waterway became less and less, but at one time it was part of a bustling industrial system and it was a mild diversion for the Peggoty workers to shout some comment, usually ribald, to the bargees as the brightly-painted vessels went placidly by.

But the cut was the scene for other activities and one couldn't work at Peggoty's for very long without becoming aware of them.

The bank was a favourite haunt of courting couples, who never seemed to know that the factory was occupied. True, the windows overlooking the water were never cleaned – that would have been possible only from a stationary barge – and anyone on the canal bank must have thought the place looked so dingy it couldn't possibly be in use. And there were rusty wire-mesh guards into the bargain to prevent energetic youngsters breaking the panes. In any case the amorous wanderers never seemed to pay any attention. And that gave great delight to Peggoty's workers. When a couple were espied in any sort of compromising situation word rocketed round the works and faces appeared at every vantage point.

Never was there a more eager audience than during the early days of the war, when somebody ran round the place breathlessly passing on the information that Little Dilly was there with a Yank. Now Little Dilly must have known she could be seen because for a brief spell she had been a real little charmer on the Peggoty payroll. She was in her late teens when I first knew her, a demure captivating brunette, with a way of looking at you from under arched brows. She didn't take long to learn there was only a meagre living to be had from mending and before she was 20 she had left to ply her trade as a lady of easy virtue. She wouldn't have had difficulty finding clients.

There was nothing brisk and business-like in the way she picked her spot with the American. They strolled along the canal bank and now and then she looked up at him in the engaging way of hers. If she knew she could be seen by her erstwhile workmates she gave no sign. Or did she? For when things could have become interesting for the onlookers she and her temporary boyfriend disappeared behind some convenient bushes, to reappear some time later. They then left their hastily arranged love-nest with quickened step, Little Dilly slightly ahead. Another client had been added to her tally and later in the day there would doubtless be more.

It wasn't only the canal bank, however, that was the focal point for such activity. One of the twisthands at that time was an old west of England character called Tim Grouter. He was one of those people who look old the first time you see them and yet of an age that you couldn't possibly be sure was right to within 10 years or so. And as the years roll by they still look as old as when you first saw them.

It was in the late 1930s when I first knew Tim. If pressed I would have put his age to be around 60. Twenty years later he might still have been taken for 60. The only difference was that his bronchitis seemed to get worse. But there was a joke in the factory that it wasn't bronchitis: it was, said his workmates, breathlessness brought on through his amorous entanglements with a certain lady who used to visit him at work, always on Fridays.

It was on one of the firm's outings that I first saw old Tim's companion. He introduced her as his daughter. That statement was made without the slightest flicker of deceit or embarrassment from either party. Tim had never earned a big wage but he had done all right by the standards of the day. No one at Peggoty's seemed to know all that much about him. He lived on one of the estates on the other side of town – the address on his insurance card supported that – and he spoke of his grown-up family. Yet, according to the ages of his children, talked about but not seen, this 'daughter' had arrived 20 years earlier than any of them. She was the flashiest, brassiest bit of mutton dressed as lamb as could be imagined. It was generally reckoned she received support from sources other than Tim and dressed accordingly. The first time I saw her she was wearing an ocelot-type coat, saucy red hat, red shoes with gold buckles and an enormous pair of earrings in the shape of tankards. It so happened that she and Tim were sharing a seat on the bus directly across the gangway from mine and I was a bit taken aback when she fished into her handbag, brought out a tin of snuff, tapped it on top in the time-honoured fashion and politely offered me a pinch before she took hers. No doubt there were times when her profession (for there was little doubt about what it was) called for a clear head, but I watched, fascinated, as she spilled a little of the snuff onto the back of her hand and, in a style that couldn't have been bettered by any of the twisthands, disposed of it.

As Tim got older his gait became slower and slower, his breathing more laboured. 'No doubt about it,' somebody said one day, 'it's Getup Gertie that's doing it.' Each Friday, just after turning-out time, she appeared at the works, and the visits had been going on for some time before Jack Preston found out. It was obvious the lads in the factory were not going to say anything about them. They didn't see any point in denying themselves what had become a fair old entertainment.

Getup Gertie turned up on Fridays, naturally enough, because that was the day Tim could hand over a bit of his hard-earned cash. It was the efforts he made to claim his dues that rocked the lads in the machine shop on the floor above. The word had got around what went on and no time was lost in boring holes that enabled the youngsters to see without being seen. At the appointed time the fun and games would begin as Tim, in his mucky working clothes, would struggle to prove he hadn't lost his manhood. From the eye-witness accounts that afterwards became common knowledge Getup Gertie's best effort was when she leaned against one of the massive machines and tried to take Tim on to its rhythm.

By just after 3.30pm the lady was usually on her way, doubtless to plough other furrows, so to speak, and Tim was left, financially worse off and gasping hard, back in the world of cotton, artificial silk, bobbins and carriages and all the bits and pieces of his working life. And you could see him, soon after his 'daughter' had left, the same old Tim Grouter you had always known, passing the time of day, asking you to reckon how many yards were left on his warp, making some complaint about the yarn he was working. The lads in the shop above might chuckle among themselves for a while but it was soon back to their machines or threading-tables. A diversion was always welcome but there was no point in it going on for too long; in the hard world of piece rates a living could only be made by steadily slogging it out.

There was a diversion one day, however, that caused me some anxious moments. Almost in passing, certainly with no sense of alarm or urgency, one of the men reported that there was a fellow who looked to be a tramp seemingly intent upon jumping into the canal from the bridge only 50 yards or so from the factory. 'How long has he been there?' I asked. 'Oh, a fair time. He keeps looking up and down the street and two or three times he's had his leg over the side of the ironwork on the bridge.' 'And you never thought fit to come earlier?' 'Well, if he wants to go let 'im. That's t'best way o' looking at it, I reckon.'

I rang the police. They would have a man along in a few minutes. Meantime, they said, I ought to go along and keep an eye on the would-be jumper. I dashed to the end of the short street where the bridge was situated. The man saw me and looked a long time in my direction. There was a look of utter resignation on his face. He leaned over the balustrade. As the police had said, it was unlikely there would be any suicide attempt while somebody was in close proximity. True to form, a minute or two later, a policeman strolled round the corner at the other end of the street. I put up my hand and he acknowledged me. And then I heard him say, in very matter-of-fact tones: 'Now then, my lad, what are you up to?' Gently he led the man away. So I suppose a life had been saved, albeit temporarily.

What, I wondered, would the twisthand who first saw the incident have done if the poor bewildered wretch had jumped? Counted the number of times he came up before disappearing completely?

Bodies *had* been found in the canal from time to time. On one occasion frogmen were searching. One of them shouted to Charlie Searlby from the bank: 'You wouldn't be tucking in so contentedly if you could see the state of the foundations.' Charlie, munching away at his sandwiches, wasn't impressed. 'They were saying that 30 years ago,' he called back. Like the rest of the folk at Peggoty's he thought the old place would go on forever.

It might have gone on for a good deal longer if there had been no war and conditions had continued much the same as they were before 1939. But the quickening tempo of the post-war period brought its problems. While the machines kept working away there was always hope and for a time all seemed well. For a number of years there was a boom. But an old generation of lace workers was dying out fast. The small concerns that had been part and parcel of the trade – together with a host of merchants who did their buying and selling from a couple of rooms located in various parts of Nottingham's famous Lace Market area – were rapidly becoming extinct. Peggoty's struggled on for a long time but the machines were not replaced when they should have been. A high proportion of the plant made plain net and that side of the business was no longer flourishing.

When the machines began to get a bit tired it seemed the bricks and mortar – parts of the factory were close on a 150 years old – began to creak and sag in sympathy. Jack Preston laughed when he said: 'Aye, we shall all finish up in t'cut.' If hasty repairs had not been carried out we might well have done, for it was reported one day that part of the canalside wall was moving. The builder was called in; a tremendously long iron rod was bracketed to one of the inside walls, a sizeable metal plate threaded on to the rod jutting out over the canal and screwed tight and flat against the suspect wall. The old place was not done for yet. It still had to provide a few experiences for the adventurous.

Like so many other factories locally it was plagued by pigeons. The bills for replacing slates mounted alarmingly and a couple of men who specialised in pigeon catching were called in. They would arrive as the day was dropping dusk and, complete with torches and sacks, disappear into the rafters among the roosting pigeons. A little time later they would reappear, each with his sack bulging with our erstwhile feathered friends. We were told the birds would be sold in a city shop but that was a story we never bothered to verify. We were satisfied that the two rather furtive characters were able to keep the pigeon problem under control.

Chapter Eight

Over the years it had been interesting to watch the progress of Lizzie Tatlow. When I returned after the war it was to find she had buried her second husband and was married to her third. 'And she's had a few besides that's made sure she didn't go wanting,' said one of the menders. 'No wonder she's buried two. She wore 'em out.' It was either that or she was unlucky because it was not long afterwards that number three went the way of his predecessors.

Lizzie said three were enough for anybody. But that didn't mean her activities were at an end. She kept on at her job but found time to look after a lodger, a muscular, swarthy gentleman who would have been useful in a tight corner. 'Gorgeous,' said Lizzie, 'but he's only my lodger.' And her wrinkled face – it wrinkled from an early age – would look even more so as she grinned and left you to draw your own conclusions.

Lizzie had been crude all her life. There was really no more appropriate word to describe her. Coupled with the crudity was a fair amount of low cunning. She had come into the world at a tough time and into a tough place, and from her childhood on needed to keep her wits about her. She had few of the attributes a girl would choose to make her way in the world, except, perhaps, abounding cheerfulness.

The last time I saw her was one busy lunchtime. Strangely for Lizzie – for I had always known her as a bundle of dynamite – she was walking very slowly and her cheeks were deathly pale. She caught me by the arm and we stopped and chatted. She hadn't been too well, she said; and then her cheerfulness broke through. For 10 minutes or more she was her old self and the laughter came easily. Over the years I remembered her as rough, generous, sly, cheerful, resilient and a product of her background and upbringing. She was a child who had to work through the 1930s. To be born into a working-class family in those days wasn't the passport to an easy life. To be born into a working-class family in certain parts of Nottingham meant life's handicapper had weighted you fairly heavily.

Chapter Nine

CHARLIE Searlby was a man it seemed natural to turn to for comment and advice. If it was anything to do with jobs about the house, engines, gardening, or the affairs of the world, Charlie could be expected to talk a fair amount of sense. At least, that was the way it seemed to me when I was a youngster at Peggoty's. I later learned to revise my opinion a bit but that didn't mean I would ever try to belittle him either as a man or a counsellor. It was small wonder that so many of the Peggoty people sought him out at one time or another.

Charlie was the 'inside' hand. That, in the lace trade, meant he was the man responsible for the efficient performance of the insides of the machines – the brass bobbins, the steel carriages, and the lead combs the bobbins ran in and out of as the lace was made. It was a highly-skilled job and he worked to fairly fine limits. He had received his training at Newton and Pycroft's. 'There were no better machine builders in t'city', he would say. 'Or anywhere else for that matter.' And then: 'I had my grounding under some of the best men in the trade. What they didn't know about the job wasn't worth knowing.' This would be said with the obvious implication that Charlie, therefore, knew all there was that was worth knowing. He wasn't far wrong.

In spite of his being lame he was tough and acted tough when it suited him. He never liked to be bested (to use his own word) and he reckoned, lame or not, he could hold his own with any man in the firm. It had long been his cry that he carried Henry Goodman, the works foreman. There is no doubt that

Chapter Nine

Henry was, to a great extent, dependent upon Charlie's knowledge and co-operation. Henry had to carry the can for anything that went wrong and if he upset Charlie there were so many ways which would have been hard to detect where a bit of maliciousness would have landed the blame squarely in his lap.

The great difference between Charlie and the rank and file was that he had a questing mind. True, he liked to air his knowledge a bit, but he was far better read than the majority of those he conversed with and the temptation must have been hard to resist.

It was one of his chief delights during the war years to sit at his bench overlooking the canal and weave his theories about military strategy. In this he was helped by watching the trains passing along the main Midland line not more than a hundred yards away. As I stood with him one day early in the war he muttered darkly: 'There's some stuff being sent north today. No doubt about it, they're preparing for summat big.' Or on another occasion: 'By 'eck lad, there's been a fair amount of troop movement this week. Most of 'em looked to me like the Tank Corps.' He swung his binoculars on their strap. 'I would reckon they've got Rommel well in mind.'

Charlie always reckoned he would have liked a spell in the army. 'Great life,' he would say. 'I'd give a lot to have a go.' Certainly he had an adventurous spirit and he had been camping to places that most of Peggoty's didn't know existed. Much as he knew about his job, it was a matter of deep regret to him that he wasn't allowed to work during the war in one of the Ordnance depots to use his skill turning out munitions. He said it was patriotism and maybe that was true, but he would also have liked to handle a bit more cash than the modest wage he was paid at Peggoty's. But there was no chance of his moving because the factory had a contract to supply netting for use in the desert to keep flies off sleeping troops.

It was during high summer that Charlie was most likely to be in his most amiable and expansive mood. One thing he would never attempt to deny: he had the best working billet in the whole of the factory. His bench was right up to the canal windows and, as the firm had no canteen – a not unusual thing even in the immediate post-war years – his dining table was where he worked. It was his practice to have a leisurely meal before leaving his working stool and settling down into a little wooden armchair for a brief nap or read.

On the rare days when it got really hot he would fling open his windows and 'lunch on the terrace' as he called it. He was a finicky man and wouldn't dream of settling to his meal without first laying out his small tablecloth and making sure the necessary cutlery and condiments were all nicely to hand. He would then take his pile of sandwiches or salad from his lunchbox and set to with relish. One particular day, warm but with a slight breeze, he had just laid out his food and was about to tuck in when there was a cascade from above and both Charlie and his lunch were drenched. Charlie's face changed from its healthy brown to violent magenta and when he had recovered enough to get his breath his language was such that even in this permissive age it is better left to the imagination. If the liquid had been rain or water from the canal it wouldn't have been so bad. But it wasn't. It was urine – and emptied from the second floor!

There was only one gents' toilet in the whole place and that was on the ground floor. It was a long way for twisthands to walk – and an arduous business to climb anything up to 45 stairs back to their machines – and so a large tomato tin did duty as a chamber pot. After use it was not unknown for the contents to be pitched from the nearest window into the canal. It was simply unfortunate that Charlie had to get the full treatment on that memorable day and go without his lunch in consequence.

If Charlie had been around today he might easily have been a union official. He was hard, he had a conscience, he was a fighter and he was all for workers uniting, while at the same time he always gave the boss a full day's work. Maybe his lameness had a lot to do with his attitude towards life but he was devoid of self-pity; certainly as far as one could judge. Maybe it was because his early married life had been troubled. There came a time when his mentally ill wife had to be institutionalised. There was never the slightest chance she would be able to take her place in normal society. Charlie, a young and vigorous man, went to live with another woman and raised a family. When at long last he was free he lost no time in legalising his affair.

It was then that he seemed to mellow and would talk for hours about what he had done to his house and garden. He became something of an expert grower of tomatoes and chrysanthemums; and when they were mastered he tried his hand at growing grapes. So proud was he that when I showed an interest he insisted I should have a go. But he couldn't hand over his green fingers and all I managed to get out of the effort was a greenhouse floor that lifted through prolific growth below ground and an article in the local paper on how *not* to grow grapes.

Charlie was the sort of bloke who could fit in with any firm's requirements provided there was a bit of machinery around. When things went wrong at Peggoty's anywhere in the plant the cry would go out: 'Fetch Charlie.' And if he was ever stumped he would make a good enough effort at putting things right to kid you that the repair was beyond the powers of any mortal.

When the old firm closed down eventually and new machines were brought in to try and start another side of the lace business, old Charlie was kept on to do a bit of work from one or two competitors on a commission basis. His knowledge of machine insides was so vast that he could earn his corn and a bit of something for Peggoty's as well. His craftsmanship was too valuable to let it go out of the trade until the last possible moment.

Lace on display: unsurpassable quality.

And the last possible moment came a good deal more suddenly than most of us could have imagined. One Friday lunchtime he had eaten his sandwiches, left his little workshop (it still gave him a view over the canal but he'd been moved from the bottom floor to the top) and walked through the mending room on his way to the toilet. He stopped and had a word or two with the girls when he came back; a couple of minutes later he was dead. He had just sat at his bench when some of the girls heard a peculiar noise and a bump and saw him slumped over a pile of bobbins, his hammer in his hand. Someone came running to the office and by the time I got to Charlie he was stretched out on the floor.

The ambulance arrived in double-quick time and when we arrived at the hospital the artificial respiration carried out en route was continued. But it was no use; the brave heart that had battled through the ups and downs in a life of joy and sorrow had given out. I was asked if I wanted to go along with the body to the mortuary. It was thought best that someone should go to see Charlie's effects checked.

The mortuary was quite close to the factory, at the rear of the police station where we handed in our keys every evening for safe keeping. I waited for a while and then a burly constable – straight out of the mould of the pre-war play – came through the doorway. He said, without the slightest trace of emotion or incredulity: 'Did you know, sir, that the deceased had a fair amount of money on his person?' And, without waiting for an answer: 'Had he ever said anything about it to you?' As a matter of fact he had. Only a week or so before his death Charlie had told me he was interested in buying a three-wheeler car. He had ridden a motorbike and sidecar for years (certainly for the 20-odd years I had known him) and he reckoned he was getting a bit too old to carry on. 'There's not enough protection in the winter for an old 'un,' he said.

The policeman had placed a number of things on the counter – a pencil or two, driving licence, a few keys; but also a money-belt from which he had taken a wad of banknotes. The notes were mostly fivers but there was the odd tenner among them. The constable started to count them. He went on for some time, his voice in the same level key, as though this particular business was enacted by him every day. He flicked the notes over carefully as he counted. 'Three-fifty, three fifty-five, three-sixty,' and on and on. He finished at four hundred and five. It is a tidy sum at any time but in those days very substantial. This, then, was the money Charlie had been saving to buy this three-wheeler. He had carried it every day wrapped in the money-belt around his waist.

Shrewd as he was, Charlie reckoned that money kept on him was the safest way to make sure it was his and nobody got at it. I had now taken over the running of the factory and one day he came to me and enquired about income tax on personal savings. What would I advise? He was cagey; I gathered the sum he was enquiring about was only a few hundreds. 'Well, you couldn't really do much better than put it into a building society. You'd get a reasonable rate of interest and there would be no liability for tax.' He looked at me in a very old-fashioned way. There were no flies on Charlie as a rule, but on this day they settled without a deal of trouble. He just wouldn't believe that he could invest that way and have tax paid by the society. There must be a catch in it somewhere. And so he continued to carry his worldly wealth around with him for the three-wheeler he was never able to buy.

Somehow you could never think of Charlie without coupling his name with Billy Spiller. On the surface they were the best of workmates. I don't suppose they had ever seen each other outside of the factory, apart from Peggoty outings. But for years they met after lunch to discuss the pros and cons of the world situation.

Each lunched in isolation at his own bench and afterwards, smokes going well – Charlie was a roll-your-own man, Billy favoured a pipe – they sat for a few moments, lightly touching on the weather, some minor event of the working day, each other's state of health, and then one or the other would interject a remark that sparked off the day's real discussion. It might be unemployment and the way it should be dealt with; the value to the country of the monarchy; or, later, when we were into the war, what Churchill should do to hasten the end of fighting in a particularly vital area. And then, at two minutes to two Billy would pick up his cushion (he always kept that in his own shop and, in any case, bringing his cushion down and taking it back was part of the daily ritual) and march off, leaving Charlie to clear his lunch things away. For staff men the afternoon's labours began at two and precisely on the stroke of the hour both wizards had abandoned their weighty roles and were working.

But the surprising thing about the lunchtime discussions was that each invariably failed to impress the other. Mention Billy to Charlie and you could easily be told: 'I've never known such a bloke for not knowing A from a bull's foot. He talks a load o' nonsense.' And if you saw Billy and happened to mention Charlie it could well be: 'Do you know, I've got to the stage where I can hardly talk to him. Honest, he spouts more drivel than any man I've met.'

The following day their lunchtime recital would continue, both of them enveloped in clouds of smoke and hot air.

Billy Spiller was one of the best warpers in the trade. He, like so many of the Peggoty men, turned up for work when he was half dead. Just about the only time I knew him to be away from work – and then only for a day or two – was when he had been fishing and, through sitting too long in the sun, had been so badly burned about the face and neck he was unsightly. His eyes almost disappeared and he stayed at home in a darkened room for 48 hours. He could easily have swung a week's absence if he had wanted, but as soon as he was reasonably presentable he was back at work.

Fishing was Billy's life outside the factory. Sundays without fishing, in season, were unthinkable and he reckoned they gave him enough health and happiness to face whatever the working week might bring. He said fishing helped a man see the world in its true perspective, was the ideal hobby, and made demands only when the participants were eager. At other times the angler could go to sleep. It was one of the sleepy Sundays that give Billy's face such a beating.

At work he spent long hours on his own. That could have been the reason he was ready for a chat when any of the twisthands went into his shop to collect a new warp. Billy was prepared to gossip. 'Nose as long as one of his fishing rods,' said Andrew Paige. 'Put a bit o' bait down and he'll do owt to try and catch what's going.' It was one of Andrew's great delights to start the most unlikely stories, tell them to Billy in great confidence and then sit back and await the results.

Billy was one of the first to put his name on the outing list when it appeared each January and when the event took place he was eager to appear on the group photograph. Old Andrew once said to me: 'I bet owd Billy Spiller's asked for a copy of the photo we had took, ain't he?' 'Yes,' I said, 'of course he has.' 'Ar well,' said Andrew, 'it's all a blind. He has one because it'd look a bit odd if he didn't. But I'll wager a couple o' bob he never takes it home. And I'll tell you why. His owd woman'd lynch him. He always cons her the outing's a fellas do. You know, without any women.'

There could have been a deal of truth in what Andrew said because on one occasion a press photograpaher came along – it was our 25th annual outing, I believe – and Billy, a few seconds before the camera clicked, slipped away from the back of the crowd and wandered out of sight behind the waiting bus. 'Sorry about that' he said afterwards, 'I thowt I'd lost me pipe.'

It was Billy's liking for a bit of gossip that very nearly landed him in trouble with Tucker Wilding, the first full-time fire-watcher we had at the factory during the war. Billy was my partner on fire-watching duty during those early days of uncertainty and one evening he had been for a pint of beer before turning in. He strolled into the little room that had been set aside for our quarters, well content with life and prepared to tell a story or two, but as he appeared he was confronted by Tucker.

''Ow do?' said Billy.

'Not very bloody well,' replied Tucker. 'And if it comes to my attention again that you've been saying owt else about me I shall rattle thi' around the ear'ole.'

Billy's mouth dropped open. He tried to say something but no sound came. Tucker stood defiantly in front of him, maybe three feet between them. They were about the same build but Tucker was a hard man and they both knew it.

Tucker didn't say any more. He didn't need to. It was one of those occasions when the air was heavy with silence. In my extreme youth I felt a bit awkward about it.

After what seemed an age Tucker said: 'Right, let's forget about it.'

Billy was more than glad to do just that. I never found out what he had been saying but there was no more unpleasantness between the two men. Which, from Billy's point of view, was a good thing. Tucker liked a drink or two but anyone with half an eye knew he would have been a rough handful, drunk or sober.

Charlie Searlby and Billy Spiller were craftsmen. It was their kind that kept the trade going. Without their expertise Peggoty's couldn't have kept their doors open. To watch either of them at work was a revelation. If something was wrong in the sphere in which they specialised it was put right without fuss or bother. Of course, one could argue that it should have been put right; that was what they were there for; that was why they drew their wages. This was true, but it was still a marvellous experience to see them at work.

But not all the Peggoty people were specialists. Somewhere in every firm, it seems, there has to be someone to do the humping, the fetching and carrying, and those concerned with that kind of work – certainly up to the time of the last war and for some time after – were usually badgered from pillar to post, at everybody's beck and call. Such a man was Walter Belling.

Walter was another of those individuals who never seem to alter in appearance. He looked a much-worn middle age when I first knew him and when I saw him for the last time, almost 30 years later, he looked just about the same. He joined Peggoty's in the middle 1920s, having worked for a time in the London furniture trade. Whether he had ever served his time as a tradesman I never knew, but he was more than a bit handy with woodworking tools and there were a few improvements around the factory that bore testimony to his skill. He had returned to Nottingham because the trade in London had gone slack and he thought he might do better back home. Home to him was a cottage near the factory, the tenancy of which went with the caretaker's job.

Walter's father had been the caretaker-cum-odd-job man for many years. He was known as Joiner Jack and he did a bit of everything – working the boiler, simple woodworking tasks, mending belts, greasing machines, humping yarn about the place, taking out rolls of finished lace to local customers.

Almost as if it had been arranged, Joiner Jack had a heart attack one summer morning. He died shortly afterwards and Walter, looking for a job, was taken on, but only on a temporary basis. He laughed many times afterwards when he recalled that the temporary arrangement was never amended, even 30 years later.

Chapter Nine

When I first knew him he was earning slightly more than two pounds a week. For that princely sum he must have worked more than 50 hours. He would be at work at six o'clock in the morning to rake out the boilers (often he had been there the previous night to 'throw a bit on and damp down'). His morning session lasted until close on midday. He would then go for lunch, to return sometime before three o'clock. He finished at six, having made sure all was well with the boilers. If necessary he would have a walk back to the works during the evening – again to 'throw a bit on'. On Saturdays he would be in at about seven and be there until midday. A bit of simple arithmetic and it can be seen he was paid about ninepence an hour, rather less than fourpence in today's coinage.

He now lived in a tiny terrace house with his wife and young son. His wife was a hairdresser with a fairly well-to-do clientele. It was just as well, for in all the years I knew Walter only once did I hear him make a protest about his lowly pay. It was in the early 1950s; his weekly wage by that time had risen by about another two pounds. 'Four quid-odd a week is no good to me,' he said. But he quickly pocketed the packet I gave him and the mood had passed in a twinkling. He got a five-bob increase now and then but it was a disgrace that a man should have been asked to do so much for so little.

Not that he looked for work or ever tried to improve his lot. He would do what was asked of him but no more. Over the years he became more and more entrenched in his rut. But it was a comfortable rut, knowing as he did that his wife was earning as much or more than he was and as the years went by he hadn't either the know-how or the energy to get himself fixed up with another job.

Every now and then he would be found sitting on a wooden platform arrangement on top of the boiler, cigarette, long since gone out, between his lips, his arms folded, his head gently nodding. The threader lads took delight in creeping into the boiler housing now and then, standing in the shadows – it was a pretty dark place – and shouting in unison when all was quiet: 'Walter!' His silhouette would jerk upright and his reaction was a sort of reflex. He would roll off his seat and make out he was scrambling about on the far side of the boiler adjusting some valve or other. And invariably he would reply, in a faraway voice he had off to perfection: 'Right, be down in a minute. Just having a bit of a job with this 'ere.' The lads had disappeared, of course, by the time old Walter struggled down.

Morning, noon and night there was a fag hanging from this lips, sometimes alight but more often not. As a variation on the trick of shouting to him in the darkness there was the day when a couple of the lads crept into the boiler housing, noiselessly made their way up the boiler steps and along to where Walter sat asleep. Then, at he appropriate moment, behind his back, they lit pieces of newspaper and flashed them in front of his face. Walter was galvanised into action but hardly in his accustomed manner. Shocked, he fell backwards from his perch into the soot and grime on the boiler top but his presence of mind didn't desert him. 'Fire!' he yelled, 'Fire! Ring the bloody bell!' By the time he had regained his feet the tapers were out and cruel hoaxers had vanished into the shadows.

I felt sorry for Walter in many ways. He would have done himself a lot of good if he had been more assertive. He would dearly have liked to have had a bit of standing and this was reflected in the way he usually had to be told twice or more to get a job done. By not responding at once he somehow created for himself a bit of an illusion that he would tackle the job in his own good time. Most of the work he had to do was menial – sweeping the stairs, carrying heavy boxes of yarn, cleaning windows, delivering pieces of lace. Yet never could he be persuaded to don a pair of overalls. That would be a bit beneath his dignity. He was a friendly soul, yet without any close friends. He liked to think he had a few bob in his pocket but it is doubtful if he ever had much more than a pound to buy his unending fags. For years and years he was a Nottingham Forest supporter – those were the days when the stars were Tommy Graham, McKinley, Pugh and brilliant Tom Peacock – but he never went to a match before half-time.

'Go the match last Saturday?' somebody would ask.

'Oh ar,' Walter would reply, 'I decided to go at the last minute. It was such a nice day I decided to stroll down.' He did and it was all part of his plan to see his favourite team. But by going along at half-time he didn't have to pay the full admission price, simply because he couldn't afford it. 'Up the Reds!' he would shout to anyone walking down the factory yard. That somehow gave him a bond with the other factory supporters, who made a habit of gathering at the Trent End, and they would have common ground for a discussion.

Just how badly off Walter was is illustrated by the fact that he was once persuaded to go on one of the firm's outings – to Skegness – and during the entire day he never took off his raincoat. That, I knew, was simply because he was conscious of what he was wearing. It was a faded green suit he had bought off one of the men at work and to have discarded his mac would have been to inform the rest of the party he had no other suit to change into. He tried to pal up with the hard drinkers in the party but they downed four or five to his one. Yet beneath it all he tried to preserve a certain bearing, somehow seeing himself as being on a higher rung on the social ladder than he could ever hope to reach.

He had a peculiar sort of pride. He had obviously been a fair sort of joiner in his time and might have been able to turn out a presentable job even when his best years were behind him. But he firmly refused to wear glasses. He would have you believe his eyesight was unimpaired even though he would fumble for the groove in a screw and then guide the screwdriver into it.

'You seem to do a fair amount of reading, young Mark,' he said to me one day. 'Now I've got a book that should interest you.'

Those were the days when my reading diet was mainly Leslie Charteris and his Saint, a natural enough progression from Bulldog Drummond perhaps.

'What is it, a thriller?' I asked him.

'Oh ar, it's a thriller all right,' he said. 'Any road, I'll bring it in for you.'

He did; it was a novel by Robert Keble entitled *Simon called Peter*. It was considered daring at the time of its publication and, so far as I can recall, it told the story of a clergyman's war service in France during World War One, relating his fall from grace. I can see now the strange light in old Walter's eyes as he gave a hint of what the book was about. He had the air of an old roué.

And that is how I picture him when recalling the time he gave me the fright of my young life. After a spell of fire-watching I went downstairs very early in the morning to the office ablutions for a wash, prior to having breakfast. I was feeling cold and cramped and glad that another spell of only half-sleeping was over. I fumbled in the darkness of the Sale Room for the light switch and staggered back when I saw the huddled figure stretched out on the table. It was Walter, startled into wakefulness. Immediately, his old brain started working. 'Bloody clock wrong again,' he said. Which, I would have staked my life, was a mile from the truth. He was a wreck from the evening before and he was not improved by the few hours he had spent on the hard table. He must have found a cheap touch somewhere (it was rumoured there was a woman living close by who could be accommodating) and after turning out of a sleazy bed in the early hours and having keys to the premises, he knew he could kip down until it was time to rake out the boiler. When I told Jack Preston about the incident he chuckled, his double chin wobbling. 'Randy old sod,' he said. 'We shall have to keep an eye on him today. He'll be flat out on top of the boiler.'

Finally, there was Walter's son. He grew from being an engaging little lad into a smart-aleck who knew all the answers. Once, in a moment of confidence, Walter said he had near enough broken his mother's heart. And his father's too, judging by the strained voice.

It will always be possible to picture again old Walter. It was he who I first heard shout the clarion call as his fellow-workers trooped out of the factory on Saturday lunchtime, with a long day's rest before them. 'Don't be late on Monday!' Over the years I was to hear him yell those words a good many times.

Chapter Ten

PEGGOTY'S could boast two of the slowest cyclists who ever worked in the lace trade. One of them was Henry Goodman. He was the works foreman and proud of it, but when he was awheel (or when he wasn't for that matter) he looked like a tramp. He wore a stained raincoat of great age, a flat cap, shapeless and sporting holes, and bike clips gripped his frayed trousers in such a way that passers-by might be treated to either an expanse of wrinkled sock or bare leg. And invariably his old pipe would be clenched determinedly between his teeth. It was rumoured he was once stopped by police because he was obstructing the highway, moving, so it was said, only fractionally faster than hurrying pedestrians. He lived some three or four miles from the factory and not only cycled to work and home again, morning and evening, but made the two-way journey each lunchtime. Altogether it was near enough 15 miles a day. He said he did it to keep fit; Charlie Searlby said it was because he was too mean to spend money on bus fares.

He always gave the impression that he considered himself a cut above anyone else at Peggoty's – with the exception of the boss. To him Henry showed the utmost deference. And yet he had no greater critic than Jack Preston. Many's the time I sat on my high stool and heard J.P. groan when he knew Henry was on his way to see him. His approach was always a noisy affair; Henry was incapable of walking without slithering and nine times out of 10 he would trip up the four steps leading from the works to the office. As the banging and clattering got louder J.P. would groan with: 'Oh God, not at this time.' That was said to indicate it was too early, too late, or simply inconvenient. But to give the boss credit he usually managed to put a brave face on things, finally smiling as he pushed Henry off, hoping there would be a reasonable interval before the procedure was repeated. And on a bad day it could have been up to a dozen times.

There was not overmuch respect for Goodman in the works. The twisthands reckoned that Charlie Searlby carried him. There was some truth in that and a few well-directed remarks from Charlie himself added weight. There was no better craftsman than Charlie and it was within his power very often to get Goodman out of trouble or to make things more difficult for him. Charlie knew the drill and was well aware that he could say a few things that would make Henry out to be a chump. Naturally, the rank and file were always glad to think their foreman knew next to nothing and Charlie, ever a master of verbal timing, seldom lost the opportunity to get in a dig.

'Do you know,' Charlie told me once, 'the first thing Goodman thinks of when he's got a machine to mend is a fag packet!' 'But,' I said in my youthful innocence, 'he smokes a pipe.' 'Ar,' responded Charlie darkly, 'I'm not talking about smoking. I mean he looks for a fag packet to pack in between the bars. There's more bits and pieces o' cardboard in them machines than there is at John Player's.'

It was said of Henry that his first job on arrival at the works each morning was to go to one of the drip-tins that stood at the end of each machine to catch surplus oil, dip his fingers in and then rub his face.

'That's just in case the boss comes in a bit early,' said Charlie. 'Then he can make out he's been hard at it. Honest, it's the fust thing he does every morning.'

But Henry had seen days of greater affluence than those he knew at Peggoty's. The story was current that he had at one time been a factory owner in his own right and had done reasonably well until a slump in the trade forced him to sell up and seek work under someone else.

He was not a well-to-do man while I knew him but he had acquired a few of the things which in those days set him a bit apart from most of those he worked with. He owned a car (and there weren't many owned by working men before 1939); he had a holiday caravan at the coast (and there were even fewer who had those); and he'd owned a couple of houses for a good many years. He didn't boast about these possessions but he let it be known he had them as a result of his own efforts.

Charlie didn't see it in the same light exactly. 'I'll tell you why he's got a bob or two. 'Cos he's too mean to spend owt. He'd skin a flea for a farthing.' And the rumour went round the factory that he'd been known to dry out once-used tea leaves, add a few fresh ones and then brew up from the resultant mixture.

'I've known some big pots in my time,' old Henry would say, and he would reel off the names of well-known financiers. 'Ah,' he would mutter, 'when I were in my prime they all wanted to lend me money. I should a' feathered my nest while I had the chance.'

I put it to Jack Preston one day. 'Yes,' he said, 'there's some truth in it somewhere. But with his mumbling and stumbling it's like trying to prise a winkle from its shell.'

Whether Henry took kindly to working at Peggoty's you never really knew. But he was another of the old school. If he ever took a day off it was because he hadn't the strength to propel his bike. While ever he could cock his leg over the crossbar and keep pedalling he would turn up for work. Traffic conditions today would have bewildered him, but with the world moving at a slower pace he was very much part and parcel of the Peggoty regime.

He was a taciturn man and in profile looked for all the world like Mr Punch. There were times when he was almost inarticulate, words and phrases getting mixed up as he blurted out his instructions. Never, as long as I knew him, did he get the boss's name right. He would lurch into the office and ask: 'Ista Mester Proston in?' Proston was a common one, but he had variations. It could be Pristham, Froston and, once, Frosby.

Henry was terrified of the telephone. For years the one we had in the outer office was the pedestal variety with a detachable earpiece and on the occasions when he was called to it he would visibly shake. Controlling himself sufficiently to grab the earpiece he would shout at the top of the stalk: 'Is that you?' And on one memorable occasion he said: 'Hello, that you? This is me.'

It was his boast that he had spent some time in Russia – and this was in the days when it was unusual to come across anybody who had ventured as far abroad even as France.

'But I'll tell you this. Wild horses wouldn't get me back there. Did I ever tell you about the time I was nearly robbed? Waited for me to drop off to sleep and then went to work.'

Henry's Russian story had been told so many times that he managed to regale whoever was willing to listen without, for him, the usual inarticulation. He had, it transpired, been over to that strange country to erect machines and his story was that just above the bed head in his cheap hotel there must have been a secret panel in the woodwork. He was a light sleeper and one night as he lay there, very still, there was a tiny click just behind his head. In the darkness he felt a hand groping under his pillow. He moved not a muscle until... 'Suddenly I had him.' There was a squeal as he applied pressure and twisted. 'If only I could have got out of bed without him knowing. But the blighter managed to get away.'

'But did he take anything? And, anyhow, how did he know there was likely to be anything under your pillow?'

'I must have dropped it out some time during conversation,' said Henry. 'Always reckoned to keep my money there. But for some reason, on this particular night, I didn't. I'd got it round my waist in a belt.'

So he kept his precious roubles and the would-be thief had a mauled wrist to remind him of a painful encounter.

As Henry shuffled his way around the works and, at the end of the day, slowly made his way home on his bike, pipe going, clad in his shabby old mackintosh, I found it hard to believe there had been a time when some loose-shirted, high-booted scowling Russian had waited near his bedroom intent upon robbing him. But Henry had an air of mystery about him and maybe the Russians were intrigued by him as much as he was by them...

The other cyclist to rival Henry Goodman was George Bainbridge. I knew George for close on 20 years and from the first day I saw him until the day he died I saw him only once without his cap and then, when he knew he had been spotted, it was back on his head in a flash. As Andrew Paige had once informed me, he was completely bald; no sign anywhere of a hair. It was well before the days of Yul Brinner and Kojak and his appearance was obviously a source of embarrassment. Even with his cap on he looked more than a bit peculiar. He had a red face, a longish nose and maybe half a dozen ill-assorted teeth, two of which were in the vampire position, so that when he laughed – and he laughed fairly frequently – his appearance could be positively menacing.

But he was a kind and big-hearted man, could tell a tale with the best of them – some, but certainly not all, risqué – and was incapable of bearing ill will. He had a story about practically everyone in the factory and when he began: 'Here, I'll tell you about the day that…' away he would go, nodding, laughing, rubbing his ruddy face, swivelling his cap about but never removing it; and by the time he had finished he'd enjoyed the story as much as the person listening. 'Not a word about this, mind,' he would conclude, when he dried the tears of laughter from his eyes. And he would never tell a story if he thought it would be passed on to the detriment of the butt of the tale.

George was a bachelor who lived alone. He had no relatives and has been dead for close on 30 years, so he won't mind if one of his stories is retold.

'There were old Henry Goodman, see. It was about half-past nine in the morning and I had to send for him to have a look at number 13 machine. Well, he comes into the shop d'you see, and I says to him: "Henry, can you make this your first job?" "First job?" he says. "This ain't my first job. I've bin here since afore eight o'clock". Well, I knew he hadn't 'cos he hadn't had time to dip into the drip-tin and put a few squats on his face. Any road I says to him: "Well, 'ave a look. I ain't had a very good week and I've got both machines standing. Number 12's all right on'y I haven't had time to cut the piece off yet. But I would like you to have a look at number 13 for me." Now, honestly, that's all I said. And do you know what? He walks down the alley, turns his back on number 13 and there he is peering at number 12. First of all he scratches his backside, shuffles about a bit and then he gets his glasses out. "Ar, you'll have to watch this machine, George; you've got a few long stitches. I'll tell you what. Run it for two or three yards and then I'll come and have another look." Well, do you know, I couldn't answer him. I was doubled up. Number 12's piece were finished. O' course there were one or two long stitches. The damned bobbins were empty! And d'you know, he put his glasses away and walked out o' the alley wi' never a glance at number 13. "Now don't forget, George, let me know when you've made another couple o' yards." I was speechless, and I let him shuffle halfway down the shop

Service at the dinner with a mustachioed smile.

Christmas dinner at the parent company. The facilities were better than at the Old Factory!

before I shouted after him. "Aye up, Henry, you owd bugger, you've been looking at the wrong ruddy machine."' And then George would look conspiratorial and say: 'Send for him to mend 13 and he looks at 12. Now, not a word about this, mind.'

George had two weaknesses, beer and horses. For a lot of his life he worked alone, machines 12 and 13 keeping him comfortably – or they would have done if he'd looked after a bit of the money he earned. He worked a long day, often from seven o'clock in the morning until eight in the evening. Now and then you would come across him eating a few roughly-cut sandwiches and swigging a can of tea, but his first port of call when he left work was the Stag and Pheasant. As the years crept by his calls became more frequent and of longer duration and there were times, so we heard, when he had difficulty making it home. But make it he did and could be seen the following morning cycling just fast enough to keep his bike wheels turning along the route he had taken Monday to Saturday and latterly Monday to Friday, since the end of World War One.

He spoke little about his life outside the factory. He was a solitary, enigmatic man. Andrew Paige, who had known him as long as anybody at Peggoty's, once told me, peering over my shoulder like a hawk ready to disappear should he be disturbed: 'He had a lass, did George, many years ago. Lovely she was and they were all set to get married. She died. A beauty she was. An' I don't think George has ever looked at another lass since. Wain't talk about her. Never would. But he did tell me once: "I'm finished but I've still got to go on living".'

George's second job when he got to work each morning was to study racing form. He would make sure his machines were going well: if they weren't he would give them his undivided attention and his form calculations could wait. But he was a good tradesman and his machine breakdowns were few and far between. When he was assured all was well out would come his papers. On a small threading-table at the end of his alley he would first of all lay out his daily, opened at the racing page. This was flanked by his specialist papers. No one disturbed him that first hour of the day. He would make various calculations in a notebook and by the end of the hour he had made five or six selections, which he would then work up into bets – singles, doubles and trebles.

A number of his workmates would give him the prescribed time and then wend their way towards his alley. It was not unusual to find three or four twisthands gathered there. Racing tips, football gossip and Tim Grouter's amorous adventures were seemingly the only things that made them disregard their work; racing and football betting could be classed almost as obsessions.

'What have you got for us today then, George?' they would ask.

George, wearing the look of a man who bore a great responsibility, would invariably reply: 'Well, here's what I'm doing. You blokes can please yourselves.' His selections were eagerly perused. There was no guarantee they would be slavishly followed; the morning meeting was simply part of the day's ritual. For a lot of the men at Peggoty's (and for a few of the women) the day wasn't complete unless some hard-earned cash had been risked on the horses.

George would enlist the aid of one of the threader-lads to take his bets to the bookie and, being a generous man, would give the lad a few coppers for going, although I've heard him say: 'You shouldn't want owt, young man, for taking my bets. Here you are wi' my selections and all you need to do is to follow 'em yourself. You'd make a capful o' money.'

'You reckon you can beat the bookies then, George?' I asked him once.

'Beat 'em! Well o' course I beat 'em. I'm not saying I win every day but over a period of time I'm well on top.'

He appeared hurt that his expertise could be doubted. Yet George wasn't a man who spent a deal on clothes, outings – apart from those run by Peggoty's – or holidays. 'Last holiday old George had,' Jack Preston said, 'was when he went with me to the Isle of Man. And while we were there war was declared. Never known him go away since.' It was a long time since August 1914, so what did George do with his money? It must have been beer and horses. And the only conclusion was that he didn't beat the bookies. It was just a bit of deception (after all, he had a reputation to keep up at the works) to say he made a profit. It was obvious unless, as some suspected, he had a fortune stacked away in his council flat.

It would be intriguing to know – and it wasn't long before we did.

George was a man of regular habits, the sort of man you could almost set your clock by. One morning he didn't show up for work. He hadn't been too

London bound to see the Crazy Gang.

well for a few days. He'd developed a cough that became more than a bit persistent. But he never complained.

'Sure you're all right, George?' I asked him.

'Right as a robin. Smoking a few too many coffin nails, but I'll be as fit as a steeplechaser tomorrow.'

I remember looking at him and feeling concerned. We had been friends for a long time – if anyone ever could be a friend with George, that is. He was a loner and too much interest was not welcomed.

But I chanced my arm. 'Look, it's time for a bit of plain talking. Are you eating enough?'

'Ar', o' course I am. Bit o' steak last night, ham and eggs the night before. And provided I can get a couple of pints on the way home I sleep like a top.'

'But don't you think that cough should have a doctor's opinion?'

'I went… see now, last Tuesday. Gave me a bottle o' stuff. 'Orrible, but I'm taking it.'

When he didn't show up for work the second day a few of us were concerned. Jack Preston said: 'Aye, I'm bothered but you know what an independent old bloke he is.'

'Yes, I know, but he lives alone.'

Jack thought a lot of him. If there were problems for George it was either Jack or me he confided in. 'Come on,' the boss said, 'let's go.'

George lived in an upstairs flat on one of the city's council estates, maybe a couple of miles away from the works. Nobody from Peggoty's had ever been inside so far as we knew. We found the place without any bother and it was a relief to see that the curtains at the bedroom window were open wide. At least the old chap was up and doing. We went to the back door and knocked, noting that the curtains there were still drawn. We knocked again, and again, but there was no reply.

'Might have nipped out to do a bit of shopping,' said Jack.

But that wasn't the opinion of his neighbour, an old woman who came to her door when she heard us knocking for George.

'Seen anything of Mr Bainbridge?' we asked.

'No,' she said, 'I didn't see him at all yesterday. And the night before he came home at half-past seven. Not like him. Comes home late as a rule and then it takes him half an hour to find his key. Often has a drop too much, you know.'

'Don't like it,' said Jack Preston.

We knocked again, much louder, shouted through the letterbox but there was no reply.

The upshot was that we fetched a policeman and watched anxiously as he broke a window and climbed in.

George was sitting in a chair by the side of a burnt-out fire. 'Must have been dead some time,' said the policeman. 'Fire had burnt a hole straight through his trouser leg. Might have set the place ablaze.'

When the flat was inspected the only bedding he had was a few old coats and there was practically no food. His possessions were few and pathetic. Nowhere was there any money apart from half a dozen pound notes and a handful of change. Dear old George, who kept a cheerful front for the world to see, who had a brave heart that pined for the girl he had been set to marry, hadn't been a racing expert after all. The bookies, it seemed, had thoroughly fleeced him.

It was cold the morning George was cremated, and a small group of his

J.P. had no parking problems in the Old Factory yard.

friends came well wrapped up to bid him farewell at 10 o'clock. It was a gloomy gathering: George had been popular, and the people there had known him for a long time, no one longer than Jack Preston. Those two joined Peggoty's on the same day and it was Jack who summed up the morning's solemn occasion. 'Aye, he was a grand old lad,' he said. 'But knowing how he liked his beer I should have thought 10 o'clock was a bit early. If he'd had the choice I reckon he'd have waited for opening time.'

George would have appreciated that.

Chapter Eleven

'TODAY,' said Jack Preston, 'Mr Bramble will be here.' He waited a moment or two until the full weight of his words had sunk in, and then continued: 'He might have a few words with you, or he might not.' I looked at him in some bewilderment. 'And,' he went on, 'I want you to be sure to call him 'Sir'. Is that clear? He's the boss – mine as well as yours. Remember that.'

And when J.P. disappeared into his office I gave due consideration to his words. Remembering my mother I squared my shoulders, pulled my jacket down unnecessarily, and found a large yellow duster I had hitherto used to polish the long desk top. Five minutes and my shoes shone. I was trying to put into practice what had been dinned into me at home for as long as I could remember: 'Look as though you belong to somebody.'

It was about nine o'clock on that never-to-be-forgotten morning and I sat on thorns. When it got to eleven-thirty I almost fell off my stool when there was a sharp rat-a-tat on the Enquiries window 18 inches from where I was sitting. I knew Henry Bramble was on the other side of the window, and with alacrity I pulled the steel rod that was there to keep out any unwanted visitors. The door was opened and I was looking at Henry Bramble for the first time. I was in the presence of a toff and, more than sixty years on, I can recall in detail that initial encounter. He was wearing a blue suit with a thin white stripe, a red and white spotted tie with a large knot between the wings of his collar, and a blue Homburg hat. His shoes shone and he was carrying a silver-topped cane and a pair of yellow gloves. Immaculate was the only description that could be applied to him.

'You must be... you must be... What-is-it, eh?'

'Mark, sir,' I said.

His eyes were fixed and unblinking and seemed to bore into my innermost depths. He didn't smile when he said: 'You opened that door and I walked in. It could have been anybody on the other side of that window.'

I was far from happy. 'Yes, sir,' I said; and then risked my life by adding: 'But I knew it would be you, sir.'

He still didn't blink. 'Oh, you did. See through frosted glass, can you?'

'Mr Preston said you would be here at eleven-thirty, sir.'

Dexterously he fished his watch – a gold hunter – from his waistcoat pocket. 'Bless my soul. Well, you were right. It seems between the two of you it's been properly worked out. Well worked out. And you're right. Eleven-thirty. That's my time.' And then, in a voice that must have frightened more than me: 'Hear that, Preston? I say, hear that?'

Jack Preston suddenly appeared at Mr Bramble's side. 'Got it worked out between the pair of you. Well, that's good.' And then to me: 'Always be on time. Makes a helluva difference. Always. Who knows, you might be manager here one day, and being on time will help you.'

Henry Bramble turned on his heel, led the way into Jack Preston's office, and in a lower voice, but one that carried along the connecting corridor easily enough, I heard: 'Might turn out alright, that young feller. Might. You never know. Give him plenty to do. Now, what's the situation?'

Jack Preston's office door was banged shut and I was left to recover, wanting to leave my stool and find somewhere secluded and safe. But I knew I might be called – and waited for the command. It didn't come, and I went on writing ticket details in the huge record book, wondering the while if I was under discussion, and whether Henry Bramble would instruct Jack Preston to get someone who was a bit brighter. Not a bad thing, perhaps, to worry a bit, but it turned out there was no need. The man I had just seen for the first time was a thorough gent. Demanding he might be on occasion, but there couldn't have been a fairer guv'nor. For the next five or six years I was to know him well.

It was told to me soon after I started at Peggoty's that he had bought the factory simply to give himself something to do in his retirement. 'Got to do something besides going from here to there,' he once said. 'Keep interested. Don't matter what, but keep interested.'

'Not many like him about,' said Charlie Searlby when talking about Henry B a few days after I had found my way around the works. 'A gent and a toff, and what's more, he knows how many beans make five.'

Henry B often made for Charlie because he was the Peggoty man who dealt with the bobbins and carriages: he was the 'inside man'. He was not slow to point out that our boss was one of the trade's experts on the little brass discs and steel holders that were vital to the making of lace and net. 'Spent a lifetime at it,' said Charlie. 'What he don't know about the job ain't worth knowing. Got his wash-leather gloves dirty many a time when he's been poking about on my bench. Can't help it. It's in his blood.'

A little later I knew that to be true when he came noisily up the stairs leading from the factory bemoaning in his loud voice: 'Done it again! Picked up a handful of bobbins with my gloves on. Damn it and blast it! Get me some hot water, young man.'

I hurried off and came back with a jugful of water from No.1 shop. (All the rooms were 'shops' and they each had a number.) Half running, half walking I found Henry B with his jacket off and the sleeves of his handmade shirt rolled high on his arms. 'Do it every time. Never learn. Pour the water in the bowl and test it. Don't want to scald myself.' So test it I did, and wondered, not for the first time, nor the last, why we didn't have hot water laid on to the little basin behind the office; and once, when I asked Jack Preston, he said: 'No need. We can manage. Always keep the jug handy.' In other words, only spend money on what is necessary.

Henry B kept a spare pair of his yellow gloves in a drawer in Jack Preston's office so that, in the event of a mishap, he was able to leave the factory

Henry Bramble as affectionately remembered. Clear-headed and forthright, he looked at the world knowing he had earned his place.

looking spry and immaculate, his suit brushed, his gloves neatly folded in one hand and his silver-topped walking stick in the other. And when he left – as precisely timed as his arrival – it would be striking a quarter to one as he started off to the famous Black Boy Hotel, there to drink a couple of pink gins with his lunchtime sandwich. That simple lunch over he was off again to another part of the set ritual of his precision-timed day. His chauffeur knew where he had to meet him, at the town end of Mansfield Road, to take him to his house for a brief nap before his afternoon plan was put into operation.

A couple of times a week (and one of the times was invariably Saturday) he went to play golf at Hollinwell, a part of Nottinghamshire that was spaciously lovely over part of the rich county coalfield. Hollinwell was known locally as the toffs' course, and many a man from the neighbourhood made a living from caddying, knowing that keen attention to a player's needs would pay off in worthwhile tips.

I never knew whether Henry B was any good at the game but, as one would have expected, he looked the part of the golfing gent, clad in plus-fours, handmade shoes, and wearing a soft brown trilby in place of the business day's Homburg.

It was said by those at Peggoty's who reckoned to know a thing or two that old Henry B was worth a mint of money. Wealthy he obviously was, for he lived in considerable comfort on the edge of Mapperley Park. He was a widower, and all the time I knew him I never found out how long he had been on his own. His house was a splendid affair, a mansion it always seemed to me, set in perhaps a couple of acres. He had a gardener of course, and on the odd occasion that I was sent by Jack Preston to get signatures on a packet of cheques it seemed to me to be a place in another world.

'Come in, boy!' roared Henry on one occasion when I turned up. 'Soon get these done. Let's see what I've been spending my money on.' I stood at the far end of his long table (a table, I told myself, that must have been set for many a distinguised dinner party) while he scrutinised the elaborately overprinted cheques and the accounts that were attached to them.

'What's this for?' he asked suddenly, and then, before I had a chance to even hazard a guess – and a guess it would have been – he went on: 'Hey well, never mind. Up to Preston to tell me that. Always check what you spend your money on and see that you get good value. Brass has to be earned. Remember that, eh?' I must have stammered something pretty well inaudible. Who could blame me at fifteen? 'And don't mumble, boy. If you don't know, say so. Never be afraid of saying you don't know. Bloody fools if they think they know everything. Some do. Met a few of them in my time.'

The weather on one well-remembered visit had turned murky and the fog had come down quickly, so much so that when I went out from that imposing room to catch my train from Nottingham Victoria – after posting the signed cheques at the main Post Office – I knew I would be lucky if I caught a train at all.

'Careful now,' said Henry B. 'Take your time and put those cheques away safely. I shall have a word with Preston in the morning. Goodnight.'

I bade him a respectful goodnight and made my way down as much of the garden path as was lit from lamps on the terrace of the house. I hadn't gone more than twenty yards before I was completely lost. I kept on going, getting more and more disorientated in the spacious garden, fighting all manner of bushes that couldn't be seen even when I walked into them. All sense of direction had gone and I wondered what I was going to do. It would be dreadful if I was so lost in that huge place that I had to be rescued – and with those precious cheques in my pocket. I turned, and through the gloom could just perceive a faint aura of light from where I had set out, and from where there suddenly came a loud voice. 'Are you alright boy?'

I was certainly not alright, but what could I do? Let Henry B know that he was employing a wimp? In my fifteen-year old inexperience, with those important cheques tucked in my jacket pocket, I maintained silence and waited until the faint light was extinguished.

'Must have gone,' I heard the old man say, and I decided to stumble on, thankful at last to reach a stone wall. I knew it was the boundary when I put up my arm and stretched my hand and couldn't reach the top. From there I inched my way around until I came to the enormous wrought-iron gates. A hefty pull, and one of the gates creaked open far enough for me to get through.

Traffic on the main road was crawling, and people were shouting, as they always seemed to in Nottingham pea-soupers. Fortunately for me I simply needed to keep on the same road. I came eventually to Victoria Station, at least having the sense to keep the cheques in my pocket that so that they could be posted safely on the morrow. But such was my concern that I wondered if I would be berated for not struggling to catch the evening post. Growing up was taking a long time.

It was on a day of bright sunshine that I saw where Henry B kept his magnificent Rolls-Royce: it was a converted stable, roomy enough to have comfortably housed a family. The large double wooden doors stood open to reveal the limousine in all its glory. It would have been a striking car at any time, but in the 1930s it was the finest I had seen. The first time I saw it on the road, with Henry B in the back, and being driven by Merrit, the package looked part and parcel of the very upper crust.

Merrit, according to Henry, was a fine chauffeur (that went without saying; he wouldn't have employed him otherwise) but he could be scathing about him. 'Never trust him; never lend him money; and never offer to buy anything he shows you.'

Merrit had to call the old man 'Sir' like the rest of us, and he had to be present in immaculate livery whenever needed. Practically every afternoon in the summer the guv'nor decided to be driven somewhere, often to his farm in Lincolnshire. He loved the countryside and the coast and, after his morning visit to the factory, to be driven to some pre-arranged place was his his idea of an idyllic interlude. Now and then his choice would be to see and walk around his acres, part of the estate he would one day leave to his two married daughters.

Every so often – maybe three or four times a year – off he would go to Cornwall, to the Tregenna Castle Hotel at St Ives. Usually he would be away for about three weeks, and sometimes, when Merrit had taken him there he would issue instructions for his return. The chauffeur would be given an itinerary while Henry B was away; maybe he would have to stay nearby to be on call; maybe he would be told to go back to Nottingham to do some previously organised job. 'And I want you here three weeks from today,' might be the instruction, 'at twelve noon.'

It had been known, when Merrit had been ordered to return to Nottingham, for the boss to be standing outside the hotel, cases ready at the appointed pick-up time. 'I was there, watch in hand, waiting for him,' Henry

B said on one occasion. 'I had told him what time to be there and he was late. I asked him what time he had started out. When he told me I informed him he was a liar. If he had done as he said he would have been there on time. He had either been late starting out or he had taken a different route. Know the way like the back of my hand. Not having it. If I order him to be there on time I expect him to be there, not giving me a lot of nonsense. So I asked him how much petrol he had put in. Oh yes, I know what had happened. He had been another way. He knows he has to account to me, petrol and all, so it's no use him trying it on. Perhaps calling on some woman somewhere eh? Never trust him. Whatever you do, don't trust him. Damn fine chauffeur all the same, damn fine chauffeur.'

When he went on his Cornish holidays, and had dismissed Merrit for a week maybe, old Henry would spend his time playing a bit of golf, sitting for long spells in the hotel gardens, or simply walking. Invariably he dressed for dinner, and mostly dined alone. His world was to change forever before many years had passed – and he was perceptive enough to know it would – but while he was able he kept to a tradition to which he had long been accustomed.

Henry had a number of sayings that he would trot out at odd intervals. 'If we didn't have rain we would never value the sunshine.' 'When a bloke's trying it on let him have his say. You don't have to believe him.' 'A lot of people are born fools. Don't spend overmuch of your time trying to convince them otherwise.' 'Time's the same for everyone, prince or pauper. There are only twenty-four hours in a day.' 'If you haven't done something worthwhile every day you've wasted it.' 'Hoping for a better day is not half so good as working for it.'

He had, as has been said of many who have climbed the ladder of wealth and influence, been through the mill. 'Oh, it ain't all been beer and skittles. Not likely. Done my share of grafting, and would do again if I had to.'

He had been round the world but didn't make a song and dance about it. 'Remember this,' he would say, 'a few problems are common to all of us. It will never be all plain sailing, don't care who you are. Can't be. Think about it. Live today; you might never see tomorrow.'

When I was reading the latest Bulldog Drummond or Saint novel I made sure it was tucked well away in my lunch-case, and not left in one of the desk drawers. Henry had a habit of pulling open a few drawers now and then, and I don't think my fiction was really his cup of tea. If *he* wanted to read it had to be factual stuff, and never did he miss an opportunity to study the *Financial Times*. Often he would make a comment after running his tiny gold-rimmed magnifying glass up and down the columns.

'See P and O are doing well.' Or: 'Butterley Company have shot up quite a bit.' He would ring his broker. 'Sell my...' and he would quote an item from his holdings; and then, often half to himself: 'That'll take me away for a couple of weeks. And if I've anything left when I get back we'll see what else I can find.' Then: 'Don't dabble in stocks and shares until you know a bit about 'em. Sometimes better to pick a horse out with a pin. Study form, that's the thing, whether it's investment, horses, or any other damn thing.'

And once I heard him say to Jack Preston: 'Just strolled through that little street running off the other side of the road. See now, what is it called?'

'Normanton Street,' said J.P.

'That's it. Used to be a bit of crumpet hanging out there so I'm told.'

In my callow youthfulness I would earwig intently. Sometimes that sort of thing was said and the two worldly-wise old chaps would forget that I was within earshot.

'Looked at those crummy little places as I went by,' said Henry B. 'Why, I asked myself, would anybody choose to go after a bit of how's-your-father there, eh? No accounting for some things, is there?'

And Jack Preston would emit one of those throaty chuckles that made Henry B aware that he was talking to a man who knew a thing or two.

'But then, most folks are a bit lacking somewhere.' And out would come more of old Henry's homespun philosophy. 'Got to try and learn a bit of something new every day. Like being on a bike. Stop pedalling and you fall off.' I decided Henry certainly knew a thing or three. As he was prepared to acknowledge, life hadn't always been beer and skittles for him (one of Peggoty's twisthands reckoned *his* father had told him he could remember when Henry had been just a little ragged-breeches nipper playing around the Meadows) but he always reckoned you couldn't go wrong if you set out to be one jump ahead of the next man.

As I got to know the old man better he said to me once: 'Never be afraid to have a go. You might not win, but one thing's for sure: you damned well won't win if you *don't* have a go. And most men are keen to get rid of their money. That's a fact. Put a carrot on a stick for them and they'll go for it no matter how much they're carrying on their backs. Perhaps you won't believe this, but I was a bookie once. Reckoned I could make more money that way than trying to pick winners. I was right. They used to queue up for me to take their money off them. Remember this: ten horses in a race and the bookie's got nine of them running for him. Eh? True. I've watched 'em from inside Tattershalls and out of it. Glorious Goodwood now. Been there many times. Nearly rode the seat of my pants through when I went on a bike. Then went in a charabanc, and after that in a landau. And a year or two after in a Rolls. Oh yes, don't harm you to struggle a bit. Just so long as you keep on learning.'

It was a sad day when I learned the old man had died. It was during World War Two and I was in Holland. He had been too old to serve in World War One, and certainly lamented World War Two.

'Right, we shall defeat Hitler and Musso, but then what, eh? Tell me that; then what? We never learn, do we? Neither men nor countries. I know, I know, we've got to teach the wrong 'uns that they can't just go on and knock anyone about who don't agree with 'em. But when we've licked 'em, what then? Eh? What then?'

I bade a silent goodbye to a great gentleman. For most of his adult life he had always had the best of everything. But he had reached his position by unremitting effort. Many of his sayings stayed with me, but none summed him up better than: 'When you've managed to get a good shirt for your own back, it's not a bad idea to help your brother get one for his.'

Envoi

QUITE suddenly, on a summer's day, there came the hour of decision for Peggoty's. All had not been well with the firm for some time and only half an eye was needed to see it must be losing money. What made the situation worse was that the plant was made up mainly of old machines; and a large percentage of the workforce had reached an age when it took unkindly to innovation. The attempt to get new blood into the place had been only partially successful and it was no surprise when the announcement came at three o'clock on a Friday afternoon that after orders on the books had been met the company would be wound up.

It had, some years before, been taken under the umbrella of another company and the future for some of us younger ones didn't look too bleak. But for an older generation it was the end of the road, a road that had started for some of their ancestors in the mid-1800s.

Those who were near retiring age were given a small financial handout; others were helped to find jobs with competitors or taken into the parent organisation. But life for any of the Peggoty people would never really be the same again.

The removal of the old machines didn't take long, and when the enormously heavy pieces had been carted away, thorough cleaning of the ancient workshops began. Eventually there was a fresh look to the place and there was a tremor of excitement when new plans were made known. Raschel machines had been ordered from the German maker, an experienced mechanic had been contracted to get the plant up and running, and a young team was taken on to work under his guidance and my management.

Raschel lace was to revolutionise the trade. Because it was possible to produce at a faster rate than Leavers it was much cheaper, and it meant generally that it was a main player in most aspects of the industry. It created its own boom and became more and more popular as better and more intricate designs became available.

Until the advent of Raschel lace Leavers bid fair to rule the roost; the development of its machine had been a slow process towards perfection. But when that fulfilment did arrive one could say that, in its intricacy and precision, it was one of the wonders of the engineering world.

It is reported that the inspiration for machine-made lace came to a Nottingham stocking worker in 1764 when he closely examined the lace on his wife's cap. He thought it should be possible to improve upon home-made fabric by making it on his stocking-knitting frame. The long journey had started.

The next great step was when John Heathcoat, in 1809, perfected the machine for making plain bobbin-net. The type of net made on the old stocking-frame was superseded; hexagonal net (still used in modern times) was a tremendous development. This, combined with an invention by John Leavers, a Nottingham mechanic, laid the foundation of the modern lace machine.

Leavers' invention perfected the twisting of warp and bobbin threads, and the final step was provided by the invention of Frenchman Joseph Marie Jacquard. Each Leavers machine had a set of Jacquard cards mounted at one end, and it is these cards, through a series of holes punched into them, that enable patterns to be made automatically.

The holes in the cards correspond to figures on a pattern-sheet, each figure in turn relating to a movement of threads as shown on a draughting-sheet and revealing the skill of the draughtsman initially responsible for creating the design of the pattern.

So it seemed that lace in its diverse forms was set fair for a long and productive future. It was decided to buy more Raschel machines, transfer those that had performed so well for our company, and run the entire plant from a more modern site, all part of the organisation that could claim to be one of the largest lace companies in the world. When the old factory was pulled down, it could be said that the firm had, in peace and in war, contributed to a proud legacy: in peace holding its own with the best in the trade; in war providing sandfly netting extensively used to keep our troops comparatively comfrotable in trying climates.

For some years all seemed to be going well. But our world, with its often changing economic conditions and keen trading trimmed to meet demand, found that much hitherto made locally could be purchased cheaper abroad. The textile industry generally began to take some devastating blows, and many firms, large and small, disappeared. Peggoty's was soon a name only, and its parent organisation had, sadly, to bow before the prevailing conditions.

I often think back to a lace trade that could have borne little resemblance to modern trading, and no doubt it was right that the old factory had to make way for a new development in an ever-changing city. Now, there is no trace at all of the four-storey building that, cheek by jowl with others of similar age, had been an integral part of a prosperous working area.

The likes of Jack Preston, Bess Skeet, Andrew Paige, Johnny Hopley, Charlie Searlby, Henry Goodman, the Mitchie sisters, George Bainbridge and so many others of their age will never return. Maybe that's as well. They wouldn't recognise the socially conscious world of today, with its handouts, amenities, holidays abroad and shorter working weeks. If their ghosts do happen to flit over the scenes of their labours once in a while they'll have to

Goodbye to all that: all aboard for a works outing in days gone by.

A day of fun away from the factory.

hop pretty lively to get out of the way of transport moving far too fast for their comfort. Their halcyon years belonged to a much more leisurely age, but in many ways it was an age a good deal tougher than ours. Yet for all their struggling, the Peggoty people seemed closer to happiness than many do now. In no small measure the long years they spent in the old factory contributed to that.